Kii

Surviving the Ruthless World
of Championship Figure Skating

KIIRA KORPI
with JERE NURMINEN

McFarland & Company, Inc., Publishers
Jefferson, North Carolina

Unless otherwise noted, all photographs
are from the author's collection.

ISBN (print) 978-1-4766-8508-3
ISBN (ebook) 978-1-4766-4657-2

LIBRARY OF CONGRESS AND BRITISH LIBRARY
CATALOGUING DATA ARE AVAILABLE

Library of Congress Control Number 2022006391

Front cover image by Elina Paasonen

Printed in the United States of America

*McFarland & Company, Inc., Publishers
Box 611, Jefferson, North Carolina 28640
www.mcfarlandpub.com*

To all sensitive and kind children
in the (sports) world, who are being
or have been maltreated:
You are not alone, and you are worthy
of love and acceptance.

The prison smells like ice rink and sweat
and feels like straitjacket and threat

It sounds like a scream for help that's stuck in your belly with a belt

It looks like creatures flying across the ice
and roses flying across the crowd

The glitter of the costumes competes with the smiles
Which is more dazzling—heavenly clothing or princess-face beaming?

Children are treated like stones
Adults try to cut them into jewels

If you remain an average rock,
goodbye—trash!

If you become a bright diamond,
hello cash!

If you lose your brightness,
goodbye—trash!

You can leave the prison at any time,
if only you knew where the keys are

They're hidden in your mind,
but so hard to find

—Kiira Korpi

Table of Contents

Table of Contents

Preface

What's the point of writing a memoir when you're under 30? I laughed to myself when the idea was first suggested a couple of years ago. Then I started to reflect on the positive impact the book might have. As the saying goes, "If not me, then who? And if not now, then when?" I realized that there might never be a "righter" moment. The number of women's memoirs and autobiographies published each year is only a fraction of those of men, and to publish the autobiography of a woman less than 30 years old is even rarer. I thought about all these things and said yes to the book project.

Making this book was rewarding, fun, and even therapeutic, but also challenging and scary. In moments of doubt, I tried to stay clear about *why* I was writing this book. When I've gone through difficult times, I've gained a lot of strength and support by reading the heartfelt and honest stories of others. With this book I hope in turn to give support and insight, and to raise awareness of the training culture around figure skating.

This book is my story, but it could also be the story of anyone who has pushed themselves to the limit. This is a story of a young girl growing up in a pressure-filled environment, of an athlete's journey to the world's top levels in the aesthetic and highly demanding sport of figure skating. This is also a story about magnificent encounters, losing and finding oneself, about being ruthless and finally compassionate. It's about love, and about being human and imperfect.

From the bottom of my heart, I thank my husband Arthur, my best friend and biggest supporter. I wish to thank my dear parents, Brita and Rauno, without whom, in more ways than one, I would not be here. I feel immense gratitude for Petra, such a wonderful sister, my lovely grandparents and my many close, dear friends. I want to extend a warm thank you also to all the coaches, persons and organizations who have been there for me during my career and afterwards. I feel a little ashamed that I haven't always been so good at responding to all the messages and letters from my fans, but they meant and still mean so much to me. Last and definitely not least, I'd like to thank all the people who have helped with the birth of this book and most of all Jere, my co-author, who from the very get-go worked with tremendous motivation. Jere challenged me intensely but compassionately and was able to dive into my inner world with astounding skill and sensitivity.

Finally, *thank you to all* whose hearts I had the honor to touch through my skating.

1

Café Pushkin

Everyone looks so happy, even Susanna, my coach. She's next to me at the table. Her eyes are twinkling with relief. A win! For a moment we've forgotten the gray November in Moscow, the battles we've had. Now it's time to celebrate. I smile a tight smile.

A few hours ago, I won the second Grand Prix gold medal of my career. Kiira Korpi—gold medalist at the Grand Prix in Paris 2010 has now won gold at the Grand Prix in Moscow 2012. Only the best skaters in the world get invited to these events and I'm the first and only Finnish skater to win the title. Now I was on my way to the Grand Prix Final in Sochi, Russia. That *should* feel really good.

Around this table are the people dearest to me: Susanna, Mom, my grandmother, my sister Petra, her boyfriend Mikko and my love Arthur. My team. Even my physiotherapist Seppo is there, slurping his borscht. My hamstring owes him this Russian feast, and so much more. I wouldn't have been able to skate these high-level events back to back without his help. I worked through the pain and now I'm a winner, right? So what's wrong with me?

To tell the truth, right after the performance I was flooded with happiness hormones, and for a second, I was ecstatic, but it wasn't long before the crash came. A dark and familiar feeling started back at the press conference. The reporters were asking so many questions, their eyes shining. They kept reminding me of the importance of that win for me and for my country. The Finnish reporters probably thought they were encouraging me, but instead they made me feel super self-conscious. Inside I was retreating into a familiar place, a place where negative thoughts ruled. No time to think, to find a calm, powerful me, because the questions and expectations kept on coming.

"How do you think you can improve your performance for the final?"

"How does it feel to be the first Finnish skater to ever qualify for the Grand Prix Final?"

How did I feel? Happy? Overwhelmed? Anxious? I don't know, but I knew I had no time to stop and enjoy. I needed to keep winning. I needed to keep getting better. At the press conference, I hid any hint of pride; I didn't want to celebrate the win too much, and anyway, the good feelings were already starting to evaporate. Why am I not satisfied? At dinner, Petra looks over at me. She's good at reading me. Could she possibly know? I've never talked about these feelings to anyone. I'm ashamed. Ashamed of my own thoughts. I order dessert. I do that rarely.

I don't often get to celebrate like this, so I try to look thankful. I smile when I'm supposed to smile, I laugh when they laugh. What's going on in my mind? I'm replaying every single "mistake" in my short program, of course. I doubled the last part of my triple-triple combination and got only level 2 in my layback spin. And then there was the loop in my free program! How could I mess up my favorite jump? Such a stupid mistake. It's true that the score was three points better than my personal best, but why only three points more? Not good enough. Not. Good. Enough. Not at all the scores I was hoping for. I should obviously be able to skate for more than 180 points.

Such an empty feeling now. Maybe I'm tired? Two competitions back to back and the trip last week from China to Moscow. Yes, that's it. You're tired. No, that's not it. It can't be tiredness. You can't give in to that even if you are. And anyway, I won, I won, I won. Why am I so unhappy?

⇛ 2 ⇚

From Cracks
into Fragments

By the winter of 2015 I looked back on one of the toughest years ever. After surgery on my Achilles tendon, I did eight grueling months of rehabilitation to make it back to top level competition. I was 26. For a professional athlete that's not terribly old, but in figure skating it's considered well past your prime. At the European championships that year, the oldest medalist was eight years younger than I was, and the other medalists were teens. I already had three European medals in the bag. Now I was making big changes in my life to stage a comeback. Besides committing to a long and tough rehabilitation, I had made the decision to move from my home club in Finland to Oberstdorf, Germany.

Oberstdorf is one of the best training centers for figure skating in Europe. There's almost an unlimited amount of ice time available and some of the top skaters in the world practice there. I had moved there in the fall of 2014 to train with my new coach Carlos Ávila de Borba. As I got older, I knew better what my body needed and formed a clear idea of the kind of coaching I wanted. I realized that my only option was to replace my entire coaching team and leave Finland. I put my life on hold so that I could focus even more obsessively on skating. This wasn't an unusual move for me, since skating was the core of my identity for years. When I moved to Germany, I was still thirsty for success. I was determined to show everyone how far I had come. The price for that was loneliness, but I was ready to pay, and I kept paying. My studies in economics at the university in Tampere were not progressing at all and my social life was at a low. Deep inside, things were getting to a breaking point, and signs of exhaustion started to crop up.

I lived alone in Oberstdorf. Right after getting out of bed, I did a

5

30-minute wake-up-program designed by coach Carlos, which included some stretching and balance exercises. After breakfast I headed to the rink where I practiced for about three hours. Naturally my training program included all the warm-up and cool-down exercises and other off-ice workouts, so I was training five to six hours a day minimum. Carlos was there with me at every practice session because I was the only skater he coached full time. The next day, and the next, and the next, the same routine over and over. The days I enjoyed the most were when I could finish up in the afternoon and have the evening off. My special treat was just to go home and watch *Homeland* or *Suits* on TV. I was addicted to those shows.

I was on a mission and didn't socialize much. For sure there were other skaters in Oberstdorf, like Michal Březina and fellow Finn Valtter Virtanen and both of their girlfriends, whom I knew from before. But I mostly wanted to be by myself. I talked with my psych coach Satu Lähteenkorva by phone. She encouraged me to mix it up a little, spend time with people. One time we all went bowling after practice. I thought that would get my mind off of training, but I couldn't relax. Everyone seemed to be having a fun time. I was jealous: I wished I could also enjoy the moment. I was constantly checking the clock, wondering when I could head back home to get enough rest for tomorrow's training. My mind was racing constantly. I've heard that anywhere from 50,000 to 70,000 thoughts go through a person's mind every day, but for me it seemed to be a lot more, probably twice that! My brain was severely overworked, constantly reviewing and analyzing my schedule, my physical condition, and my skating.

I was exhausted and jittery and about to cry at any moment. I could not appreciate any progress I made. I emphasized the negative. My goals had gotten so unrealistic that even a small setback, like a "popped jump," felt like a massive failure. A popped jump is when you go for three 360° turns in the air and you do two or even one. It does happen in practice, and you're supposed to move on, but in my mind I couldn't move on. Satu said that my voice sounded stressed and exhausted, but I ignored that. In my mind, I was an elite athlete, and my job was to prepare myself for the world championships in Shanghai. I had worked on my Achilles tendon for so many months that I could never have forgiven myself if I pulled out of the competition when I was so close. Besides, we were committed to our plan to add more difficult elements to my programs after the European championships—otherwise the technical scores for my jumps wouldn't be high enough for a top placement.

My mind often wandered back to the previous few months and the fabled "comeback." Earlier in the year, at the European championships in Stockholm (January 2015), I was back after a three-year break—that's how long I had been sitting out because of various injuries. The Finnish media was excited. The headlines read "Is It Kiira's Turn?" and "Ready to Shine." I knew I was still not 100 percent at Stockholm since the Achilles tendon surgery had been only seven months earlier and my programs didn't feature the toughest jumps. Still, I performed almost perfectly in the short program and the only little mistake was in the landing of my double axel. But then again, I lost to Russia's Elena Radionova by more than seven points, which is a lot. The big gap between our scores was partly due to the fact that I wasn't able to do the triple-triple combination yet, which by the early 21st century had become a must in ladies skating. I had landed that combination for the first time in a competition almost ten years before, but due to the recent surgery I still hadn't managed to do it consistently in practice.

After the short program I was in fourth place, still in good position. Back in Finland people had already started to talk about my chances to medal. Soon after the short program I started to feel ill and called Carlos. Was it just nerves, or was I getting sick? A stomach bug hit me the following night and I had to withdraw from the competition. That was the only championship-level contest I had ever withdrawn from. My illness seemed to be bad luck, but I think it was a sign. My body was saying, "That's enough now!" But I wasn't listening to my body, nor to anyone or anything else besides my hyper ambitious, hyper critical inner voice.

After Stockholm I only had a short recovery. There I was in Oberstdorf, as single-minded and unrealistic as ever. I had some big goals. There were two months between the European and world championships, and I wanted to be able to add at least a triple toe loop-triple toe loop combination to my programs. It became an obsession. Sometimes in practice I managed to successfully execute it, but the consistency wasn't good enough yet, but if only I could do it, what a big point gainer it would be! Also, the overall level of my training and skating wasn't improving the way I had been hoping. I told Carlos I was feeling depleted. At times he did sound sympathetic, but we both knew how close the championships were and we pressed on. The atmosphere in practice was tense. I tried to hide my ever-growing anxiety. I guess we *both* wanted to show the world how far we had come. And this put all the pressure on the Shanghai event.

I had met Carlos Ávila de Borba for the first time in Lake Arrowhead, California, in 2013. This Portuguese-born coach had worked in Germany and Japan with some skaters who later became world championship medalists, including Carolina Kostner and Mao Asada. In Lake Arrowhead Carlos was in charge of off-ice training for the American skater Adam Rippon, now a super celebrity.

Carlos has also had clients from tennis, soccer and other sports—nowadays he may even be coaching a toreador. Carlos has never been a figure skater himself. He is a coach who doesn't differentiate so much between on-ice and off-ice training. There's just training. Lots of it. Before me he had never been the exclusive head coach for a skater. There had always been another coach with him responsible for the on-ice technique, such as when he worked with Rafael Arutyunyan in California. Although some might have doubted Carlos' understanding of jump technique in figure skating, I think he actually understood it very well. That wasn't the issue. The issues were in other areas.

"Carlos is a great guy, but very intense. Just train with him in short periods," Rafael warned me.

In my usual hardheaded way, I didn't believe Rafael. I was sure I could handle even the most demanding practices and intense coaching relationships, because Carlos' achievements were special, and I wanted to be part of something special.

In California I was immediately impressed by Carlos' professionalism and charisma. He did comment on other people's skating harshly, but I tuned that out at first. In the early days, Carlos was always polite and charming to me, and my parents liked him as well. He always remembered to ask how my family was and was a lovely host at the dinners he held for us. I admired the confidence he seemed to have in everything he said and did.

Carlos assured me that his innovative methods would help me improve greatly. His words hit home. I desperately wanted to become a better skater. I wanted to recover from injuries and show myself and everyone else that all the effort and sacrifice had been worth it. I adored Carlos. There seem to be a lot of coaches like Carlos in figure skating. They usually have such strong and attractive personalities that they mesmerize the skaters they're coaching. They're usually a big hit with parents, too. And young skaters, who are thirsty to achieve their dreams, believe in their coach without question. I was like that, too.

We began to work more intensely in the spring of 2014, and he influenced my training in many good ways. During our partnership there were long periods when I was injured and then there was the slow recovery of my badly torn Achilles' tendon. Even so, I learned from him how creatively you can practice even while rehabilitating. I got on the stationary bike with a big cast on my leg, did aqua jogging and even danced my programs in the swimming pool. I'm pretty sure people thought I was crazy when I tried to "skate" in the public swimming pool, but I was fine with that. Carlos showed up to each session well prepared and expected the same from me. I learned you have to always give your best at each training, no matter what. He said you can always find ways to practice even when you can't move at all, in which case you are still able to visualize or at least blink your eyes. I learned a lot of good things from him. I also learned a lot of bad things.

In Oberstdorf in the spring of 2015, after a year-long intensive training period together, our coaching relationship was no longer healthy. Carlos had begun to emphasize how I should go more boldly into my jumps and not be scared of "popping" or falling. But when I attacked my jumps more daringly and fell, Carlos seemed shocked. My body was simply not ready, and his advice was increasingly contradictory. Maybe he thought I lacked mental strength if I failed in practice or competition. According to him, I didn't know how to handle pressure. I started to believe that and was convinced that it was all about my insecurity.

One time I dared to offer a little suggestion. I thought my muscles didn't feel explosive enough and that's why I couldn't jump high enough. When I suggested we could do more exercises for fast twitch, he got angry that I would challenge his methods. He became critical of my weight, something I was very self-conscious of, even obsessive about. I was so intimidated that I felt I had to apologize to Carlos for my comment about adding explosivity training. As a result, what should have been a relaxing weekend with my boyfriend was ruined as I strived to drop a few ounces. Naturally weight counts in a sport where you need to send your body into the air. But what I now know about training is that there are also many other aspects that affect jump technique. And I was already stressing about what I put in my mouth. When Carlos and I ate lunch together I felt so anxious about eating one more piece of bread or a potato. I usually didn't, and my calorie intake was way too low for the amount of exercise I was doing. This dysfunctional attitude toward food was something I had struggled with earlier in my career, and here it was, back again.

One day in the middle of practice on the ice I got a cramp in my hip flexor. Naturally I was annoyed by the cramp because I knew how close we were to the championships in Shanghai and there could be no time to waste. As soon as I felt that ominous twinge, I went straight to the dressing room to wait until my hip felt better. When I returned to the ice just a short time afterwards, Carlos was gone. The next day he gave me an earful on how outrageous my behavior had been—I had turned my back to him and left the rink without his permission. He said how offended he was, how disappointed he was in me. I meekly listened, although I thought it was very strange and illogical. I was the one who experienced the distress in my hip and the frustration of a missed practice, but my coach made it all about him.

In Oberstdorf I began to reflect on my deeper values, those things I had compromised in order to achieve my sky-high goals: health, family, love, my natural optimism and appreciation for the people around me, and my pure love for skating. Was I living up to my beliefs, my priorities? Health was number one on the list, which I guess was quite rare for a young person. I was always either hurt or recovering physically or on the verge of a breakdown mentally and emotionally. Also, I barely saw my boyfriend or family. I felt lonely all the time—so the values of love and family were on the back burner, too.

I needed other things to occupy my mind, and a few weeks prior to the world championships I traveled from Oberstdorf to Finland. I stayed with my sister Petra in Helsinki. I needed to be in a place where I could breathe and think more freely. I badly needed a mental break from training. Petra told me she would come to Shanghai, along with her fiancé, to support me. Like so many times before, Petra was there when I needed her.

2. *From Cracks into Fragments*

A few weeks before Shanghai Carlos commented on what great timing it was that my body finally looked leaner and more toned. Toned? I had been sick for weeks and had lost all my muscle strength. I was also emotionally fragile. When we got to Shanghai and started the official championship practices, every spill felt like a massive disaster. My ability to focus was non-existent and my self-confidence completely evaporated. From the outside my practices might have looked decent, but the panic inside me was building. How had it come to this?

Rinkside, Carlos' expression was often worried, and I became extremely annoyed by all his comments. I had suppressed so much anger and resistance toward him that it felt downright horrible to go to the boards to listen to his advice. I detested particularly the comments that started with the words "If I were you...." Also, it was really starting to bug me how often he talked negatively about other people. But I also detested myself for falling deeper and deeper into a negative and fearful headspace.

On the night before my short program in Shanghai I couldn't fall asleep. I was always nervous before a competition, but with the intense exercise I rarely had trouble dropping off. In Shanghai I just wasn't able to. I made the room pitch black, put earplugs in, but even the sound of my breathing was disturbing. As I was lying in the bed, I wished I could silence the breathing sound I was making. Steady, but too loud—I was so annoyed by it. Finally, I resorted to a sleeping pill. I had only done this twice before a competition, and both times I bombed miserably.

"A Day in the Life." We had chosen this Beatles song for the short program, and oh, what a day it became. I fell on my first jump, a triple flip, which was supposed to be a combination with a double toe loop. I continued to spin decently, but then even on my favorite jump, the triple loop, I slipped from the takeoff edge. Just a single loop. An absolutely ridiculous attempt. I lost all control; I couldn't feel the ice and didn't recognize myself while I was doing my step sequence. I felt as if I was looking at myself from above. It was crazy. This was a moment I've thought about often. If that's Kiira Korpi skating on the ice, then who's the one observing her?

After the program I thanked the Chinese audience by bowing in four directions. Then I glided over to the kiss and cry corner after picking up a small stuffed animal on the ice. While Carlos and I were waiting for my scores, we sat far away from each other. I guess unconsciously we were already parting ways. Carlos had always made it known that he never got nervous in competitions, because he knew he had done a tremendous job. There on the bench that day, he didn't say a word; he was just nervously fiddling with a water bottle.

"Kiira Korpi has earned a total segment score of 41.11 points," said the announcer.

The lowest score of my entire championships career. But because it was still early in the competition and there were still a lot of skaters to go, maybe I'd qualify for the long program after all. They would choose the top 24. I secretly wished I wouldn't make it. I knew I could not have skated one more program because I was burned out and utterly empty. I didn't end up qualifying. I placed 31st, which was my worst ever result at the world championships.

I had to go through that total meltdown before I started to realize how terrible I was feeling in my relationship with Carlos. After all our intense work together, after all the hopes I had with this top coach,

Ladies short program at the 2015 ISU World Figure Skating Championships, Shanghai (Elina Paasonen / Aamulehti).

the end result was that he made me feel that I would never become a great skater unless I changed as a person. I wasn't in charge of my own thoughts or emotions anymore. I did just about everything to please Carlos. Even the slightest criticism landed like a massive personal attack. Carlos demanded that I live more lightheartedly and not care about other people's opinions about me, yet at the same time, he expected me to do everything according to his ideals. Carlos said he didn't believe in yelling or coaching through fear and was proud of that, but the way he questioned my way of doing things—and quite frankly my way of just *being*—was frightening and somehow even worse than yelling.

In that period my mind was filled with darkness and doubt, and I knew it, but I was afraid to face myself, because I was afraid that everything I had built would come crashing down. I was in denial: subconsciously I detested the situation I was in, while my conscious mind tried to reassure me that everything was great, he was great, and I just needed to push harder and everything would work out. I never raised my voice to Carlos, but I felt raw, exhausted, drained of will and energy and joy. Wasn't this what Rafael had tried to warn me about? After the dreadful competition in Shanghai, Carlos kept repeating two things: we just needed more time to practice, and I should pull myself together mentally. I was still too intimidated to challenge this. Speaking to Japanese journalists after the Shanghai competition, I kept talking about the 2018 Olympics and minimized my current crisis: "The comeback season was a little hard for me. I just need more time to practice."

Back then I still didn't understand how the disastrous performance in Shanghai had completely broken my sense of self as a skater, a self which had been the basis of my whole identity for so long. Only afterward did I realize this and how much work I needed to do to transform my outlook and my life. It was shattering. Five months later I announced that my competitive career was over. I had been skating for two decades.

Waiting Is the Worst

There's just too much time to think about the performance and everything that might go right or wrong. The nervousness and excitement are too much. I'm so anxious. The excitement is like hot lava flowing over my body and mind. Nothing can stop that flow—it covers everything. I try to eat, I try to sleep, I try to get my mind off the competition. Sometimes

Kiira Korpi

I wish I could just curl up under a blanket, hide and escape, most of all escape my own expectations. It feels like my whole life is on the line, and nothing else matters.

At the rink I just want to be on my own and keep moving. I'm worried about how to keep my body sharp and ready. I try to fill my mind with the music. On the ice, I become electrified when I get to move and glide. The moment is here. I try to feel the ice and get into a good vibe. I shift my weight from left to right. I hope that the nerves don't end up in my legs. When the legs freeze up and get heavy, numb and slow—that's the worst. But now I hear the cheers. I am energized and these insecurities are wiped from my mind. The bigger the crowd, the better it feels.

A few easy warm-up jumps, and then I mentally map out the most difficult elements of my program. The right timing of a jump depends on milliseconds, but I know how it's done, I've done it thousands of times in practice. The most important thing is to stay in the present moment. Here and now. I glide to the rinkside to my coach and grab her hand. We look each other in the eyes, the crowd awaits. One element at a time, she reminds me, and then I wait and need to hear her last, few, good words: "Enjoy it, Kiira." Then comes our thumb game—mustn't forget that! I demand that superstitiously from my coach every time. "Next to skate, Kiira Korpi, Finland." Our thumbs touch.

My thinking is clear and the feeling in my body is as sharp as it gets. All the pressure and focus come down to this moment. Like a racehorse waiting for the start, I glide on the ice and take my opening position. My heart is beating fiercely. The music begins.

3

The Gold Tap

Pony panties and elephant panties. A pair for me and a pair for Petra. The pony panties my big sister got are much nicer than my elephant panties. I want those. Please, please, please. No, wait a minute, maybe not. Yeah, the elephant panties are better than the pony, I want those. Let's change. Or what if I want them both...?

"Mom!"

"What now, Petra?"

"Kiira put both panties on!"

I was standing at the bottom of the staircase in our little house, grinning and wearing two pairs of panties. I was three. I pointed to the basket filled with dirty laundry and told my five-year-old sister, "You can get your panties there!"

Weekday mornings in the Korpi household at Aarikkalankatu 4B were a hassle. My mom loves to tell stories of my little rebellions. As she tells it, I was quite the case, a reckless, stubborn girl who loved pranks and who had an *extremely* strong will. Mom says that when I was very young people called me *Kiukku-Kiira* (angry–Kiira) and *Kalju-Kiira* (bald–Kiira) because no hair would grow on such an evil head.

Mom also likes to tell how easily I would throw tantrums if we entered the store from a different door than the one I wanted. I'd start yelling right away if we took the elevator when I wanted the stairs. And how many times did Mom have to leave a full shopping cart by the cashier because there was a screaming little girl who had to be hauled out of the store? These are the stories my mom loves to tell.

My nanny Raili tells the story that one day she tried to put some clothes on me, and I started raging, tearing them off. I was soon butt naked in the nursery yard. Fortunately, that tantrum took place on a summer day. I'd also start crying for no reason at all, just to find out how

15

loud I could be. When Dad came home to one of my rages, he always had the same questions.

"Did Kiira get enough to drink?"

"Of course!"

"Did she get enough to eat?"

"Obviously!"

"Then we need to take her to a neurologist."

Dad's patience in these situations was close to zero, and so was Mom's, I think. Mom says there were only three people who could get along with me when I was little: her, my grandma Eeva, and our neighbor Ninnu, who often helped Mom by taking care of us during my dad's long and frequent coaching stints away from home. Ninnu knew exactly when Mom was at her breaking point. That's when she would grab us and go outside.

I was a demanding child for my mom, for sure, but Ninnu tells me that she never found me all *that* challenging. For her and surely for many others I was just a very energetic little girl.

Kiira could scream for one hour if we entered a building by the "wrong" door. But I never gave in to the will of this young lady. I think that if I hadn't managed to break Kiira's fierce will, she might have grown up to be selfish and complacent.—Brita Korpi, mother

At one point Kiira's temper started to be quite impossible. I remember when Mom once dragged Kiira fully dressed into the shower to calm her down. And once she threw her skates out the window.—Petra Korpi, older sister

I was born in the middle of ice hockey season in September 1988 in Tampere, Finland. Earlier that year, Dad had just won his third consecutive championship title with Tappara, the hockey team he was coaching. He became the head coach of Tappara in the late '70s and went on to work with many different teams in Finland and internationally up until 2000.

Comparing our number of national championships, my five titles beat Dad's four. But on the Olympic level he surpassed me when he led the Finnish women's ice hockey team to a bronze medal at the Nagano Winter Olympics in 1998. Dad also coached the men's national hockey team. He's still a respected figure in Finnish hockey even though he hasn't coached in years. When I was an up-and-coming skater, I was known in the media as the daughter of Rauno Korpi, but later it turned out to be the other way around.

3. *The Gold Tap*

It was the love for team Tappara that brought my parents together, and we were all totally Tappara fans. When she was a young woman, Mom was studying to be a schoolteacher in Hämeenlinna. She got a job at the Tappara PR department to make some extra money. Sorting tickets into different piles wasn't exactly Mom's idea of PR work. Then one day she ran into a short lad who seemed strange but kind-hearted. My big sister Petra was born five years later. In the fall of 1988 Mom had to tolerate the apologies from people at the ice rink when a second daughter was born—another booking clerk rather than a future Tappara man.

Growing up I spent so much time at the rink, and ice hockey became a very dear sport to me. Petra and I would grab Dad's flipchart and draw our own offensive patterns. We couldn't understand why the good old wrap around goal wouldn't work every time—you just skate behind the net from one post to the other and put the puck in it. Somehow Tappara succeeded without our strategic input, but we loved them anyway. Years later, when I got my first cell phone, I would call home from my competitions to report on my successes, but first things first. How was Tappara doing? My favorite player was the legendary Janne Ojanen, the all-time leading scorer in Finland's *SM-liiga* (national league).

I loved watching all sports and I could easily recite the statistics of the *SM-liiga* as well as basketball, tennis, soccer and of course Formula 1. Formula 1 was my favorite, especially when Mika Häkkinen was still driving. I watched all the races and was so nervous before every single start. When Dad was coaching a team in Switzerland around 2000, the letters we wrote to each other were usually about one thing and one thing only—Mika's chances of winning the world championship title. All the personal stuff had to wait.

I had incredible determination as a child. When I was four years old all I wanted for Christmas was a *kraana*. That's a water tap. Yes, my very own water tap, not a faucet but a tap. And yes, it had to be golden. We were living in Turku, where Dad coached TuTo. At home in Tampere we used to wash our hands under the "*hana*" (faucet). At kindergarten in Turku we used to wash our hands under the "*kraana*" (tap). I had to have one! Mom reassured my grandparents that I would forget about the *kraana* and would accept a normal gift as soon as the Christmas catalogs arrived. But as the months went by, I never gave up on my golden *kraana*.

Petra tried to get me excited about some other toys in the colorful pages of the catalogs we got, but I wouldn't budge. Finally, my grandfather, a retired plumber, found a bronze tap, which he buffed until it sparkled, and that's what got wrapped up. I was so proud of my very own *kraana*, and I took it everywhere. It never left my little hands for the whole Christmas holiday. I even took it to the rink. Later, other non-negotiable Christmas wishes were a washing machine, sugar scissors and sugar tongs.

I wasn't just strong-willed; I was also determined to be different from other kids in every way. In school one day we had to simply copy a drawing of a squirrel. I changed the position of its head so it stared in the opposite direction from all the other squirrels drawn by my classmates. At birthday parties I picked the vanilla *Ville Vallaton* ice cream cone when everyone else picked the pear-flavored one. I loved the pear-flavored ice cream, but no way was I going to go along with the crowd.

As Mom tells it, she naturally gravitated to the single parents at parks, playschools and public swimming pools, because she too was so alone with her children. Besides Ninnu our nanny, Mom got some help from her parents, Eeva *mummi* (grandma) and Jussi *pappa* (grandpa). When we were little, we didn't spend that much time with Dad's mother Ruut *mummi*, but as we got older, Petra and I became really close with this independent, opinionated woman. When I was born, Dad and Mom had planned to name me Linda but then Ruut *mummi* questioned why all their kids had to be named after kitchen cabinets (at that time Petra Kitchen and Linda Kitchen were well known brands in Finland). Years later I was a judge on the Finnish version of *Dancing with the*

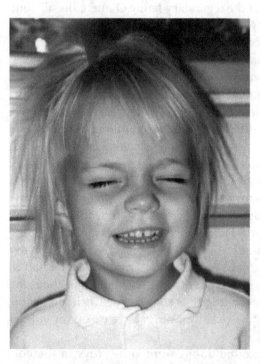

Me, a stubborn and funny four year old.

Stars. Ruut *mummi* was upset about the low necklines of the present-ers' dresses and let us know that she stopped watching after the first episode. Ruut *mummi* is over 90 now and going strong.

Mom has always been our family power figure and she is an extremely strong-willed person. I admire her persistence. She was the head of our family partly because of her character and partly because Dad was away from home so often. I don't doubt that Mom had a hard time running the family from day to day, it must have been very challenging for her. Even though my Dad worked a lot and wasn't always so present, my relationship with him has always been much less complicated than with Mom. My dad has a beautiful way of making people feel comfortable, listening to them and seeing the goodness in them.

Mom was an educator and was very strict about manners. She stressed proper behavior and self-control. When we went to someone's house, we couldn't get out of the car without being super clear that we had to shake hands with all the other guests and then thank the host for the meal. Mom got upset when one year into junior high school my score for "ideal behavior" dropped from a perfect 10 to an 8. I had helped my skating buddy Krista during a pop quiz by letting her look over to my desk and see my answers. Mom didn't stay angry at me for very long because she appreciated my friendly intentions.

Friday was cleaning day. Petra and I had to do most of the work, and we never received any allowance or special treats in return. Mom didn't believe in rewards for something that all children naturally have to do. The only way we could earn even a small allowance was to read books that hadn't been assigned at school. Mom was deadly serious about homework tasks. One Friday evening Mom burst into a rage when she came home and saw that nobody had cleaned up even though we had been home the whole day. She snapped: "I work so hard for you all and you can't even clean the house!"

"Mom, we're sorry, so sorry…"

Petra apologized and hurriedly started to dust the furniture. Dad was also quick to pick up the vacuum. I, on the other hand, plopped down on the couch with my legs and arms crossed and calmly stated: "It is you who has raised me to be this way."

I don't remember what was shouted after that, but I do remember Mom's face turning bright red and that she yelled so loud that probably even the 80-year-old couple next door started cleaning their house. Not me!

Kiira Korpi

My parents never budged on the cleaning routine. When Petra moved to Vaasa for college, she'd be back home every few weeks. Dad would greet her at the door with a vacuum cleaner in his hand. I didn't get any reprieves from housework even when my training schedule started to expand in the early days of my career. Mom insisted that we do our schoolwork, visit our grandparents and complete our tasks in the house on schedule.

Mom has told me it was difficult to raise two daughters who were so different from each other. Petra was a sweet, obedient and nurturing big sister who'd grab the cleaning rag immediately if asked. I was a stubborn child who could not be managed without a fight and could cut my own bangs if I were in a mood. Little by little, though, Mom managed to break my will and I didn't fight back as much. Sometimes Petra was overpowered, too, by both Mom *and* me. On those rare occasions when we had treats, like Jacky Makupala puddings in the fridge, I ate them so fast that Petra didn't even make it to the kitchen before they were all gone. If Mom said the bathroom was free and it was Petra's turn, I'd rush in to sit on the toilet with my pants still on, just to get there before her.

Me (left) and Petra, four and six years old, 1993.

3. The Gold Tap

Petra and I fought sometimes, but we were best friends, too. When we wrestled, she took care that she never hurt me too badly and ran to get a bag of frozen peas from the freezer if I got a bruise. I looked up to Petra and wanted to do everything she did. If it hadn't been for her, I probably would never have started skating. We've always been involved in each other's lives. Petra is still so incredibly dear. She has traveled to more of my competitions than anyone else in the family. She is so mindful of the people around her. I would have forgotten my grandparents' birthdays practically every year if not for Petra. She maintains a close circle of friends, which I didn't have for a long time. When I was younger, I was thankful that she invited me to hang out with them; I was able to at least get a glimpse of what a normal life for a young person could be. Also, Petra is a natural athlete; she's still if not more agile then at least more flexible than I am.

In my neighborhood, the kids practically lived outside, no matter how cold it got. When I started school at six, I would walk one mile to school and back every day. I usually went with Elli, my friend next door. Sometimes the walk back from school took us two hours because the little forest we had to cross was too enchanting. And I was so driven in so many ways. Even if there wasn't anything going on with the other kids, I could always smash the tennis ball against our garage door, challenging myself to break my own records over and over and over.

I couldn't stand losing at anything. Every game was a death match to the bitter end. Mom told me that when we lived in Austria where Dad was coaching one year, we used to play a dice game. I won every time because I cheated as much as I could. I was four.

When I turned ten, we were given fishing rods. We loved to go fishing with *mummi* and *pappa* at our summer house in Lempäälä. Within minutes, Petra caught a fish. Even though it was a poor little wriggly thing, I was furious. I was convinced that there was something wrong with my rod. My big sister switched with me, but then she immediately caught another fish—with my rod! My face must have been priceless to see when it turned completely red.

I never played traditional girl games; they just weren't my thing. In my first skating competition I was wearing only a practice dress, which was very plain. My coach Maare informed my parents that Kiira had made it so far up the leaderboard that she would need a real skating dress with finer fabric and sequins. Not quite my style yet! If I had to dress up for a costume party, I wanted to be a bogeyman, gangster or warrior.

Later I started to wonder about all these stories of my childhood, how I was and how I wanted to be. Do these memories come from *me* or from listening to others tell them? I've heard Mom repeat these stories of me as the obnoxious and tomboy-like child so many times that it gives me a heavy heart. How much do I really know of my early life? To what extent have I learned to see my childhood through Mom's eyes? Was I really that bad of a kid? And if yes, *why*?

My friend Elli went to the same school as me and skated in the same training group. I loved going to her house. Her dad was a priest, but their home felt so relaxed and loose. I especially loved that you could always find chocolate puddings and other treats in the fridge.

> Childhood for our girls at home was a life filled with love, limits and routines, which I didn't have much influence on. It was Brita's thing. Afterward I regretted not being more present in the daily life of my daughters because I was a workaholic. I discussed that once with a child psychiatrist who said that I can never get that time back, but the girls didn't lose as much as I thought. Only I did. That right away comforted me.—Rauno Korpi, father

Mom may have had trouble with my stubbornness in my early childhood. When I started Pellervon ala-aste (Pellervo elementary school), she saw as if for the first time some new aspects of my personality. But first she had to deal with me when I found that I was being enrolled in school.

"What on earth are you screaming about now? Why don't you want to go to school?"

"I can't read."

Elli had already learned to read, and I was determined not to be behind the others. I apparently grabbed Petra's spelling book from her room and learned to read by myself in a week. Again a familiar tale in my family, but Mom's story may have some truth in it because school was easy for me right from the beginning. I had an excellent memory and things just stuck in my mind. For exams I would study by casually turning pages and let my photographic memory go to work.

At home I had my famous temper, but in school I was a teacher's dream. My energy was channeled into something other than anger and resistance. In first and second grade we had a lovely teacher, Kaisu Seppä, who let us play with pillows or jump on trampolines during breaks. We also had real parakeets in our school that we could take care of. We made "math huts" under our school desks where we did our exercises. My parents never had to get involved in my homework, and I never stressed much about school. In high school my average grade was 9.9 out of 10 and I walked out of the graduation ceremony with honors and a scholarship. At home, though, I was warned that I had to always act modest and discreet.

> At home we never hyped the successes of Kiira or me, especially to other people. Kiira was crazy good at school, but those reports with straight 10s were hidden so that other people wouldn't see them. I have a feeling that Kiira longed to be at least a little bit cheered on and celebrated at some point also at home.—Petra Korpi, older sister

Petra and I were happy that Dad coached Tappara, but Mom was not always so thrilled. Sometimes Dad's job led to some very scary situations. There were times when we got some threats over the phone, usually from die-hard fans of the Ilves hockey team, Tappara's main rival. Most of the calls were harmless. There was one stalker who said that he knew what kind of stroller Mom used. Another time the police showed up at a game and said they needed to take Dad home. Dad jokingly asked if they were going to put him in jail in the middle of the game. The police were not laughing.

"Is your wife in the audience? Could they make an announcement to tell her to come here?"

"What's going on?!"

"Your nanny Kirsti called the police. Someone called in a bomb threat."

Now Dad was worried so he asked the police to go over to our house to watch the rest of the game with the nanny. Thankfully, no bomb was ever found, but the occasional prank calls, threats and blasts of hate toward our family were nightmarish for Mom. Dad's jacket might be wet after a game from all the spit from Ilves fans. Mom wanted to keep me and Petra as far away from all that as possible. Even long after Dad's days of coaching Tappara, Mom didn't let Dad and me to do any interviews together because she didn't want the public to associate us with him.

> Those were horrible experiences for me when someone called our home and threatened our children. That's why we insisted on keeping the girls away from all the publicity. We wanted to lead a normal life! That was a scary and distressing time for me.—Brita Korpi, mother.

Dad was a workaholic, something he admits, and work is still important to him. He gives talks at various companies and organizations about leadership, communication, and well-being at work. Dad has expressed that working a lot and being away from home has been a way for him to manage the challenges of home life and his inner life.

Mom always told us how super happy our childhood was. It has taken me a long time to come terms with the fact that in many ways it wasn't as happy as I was led to believe. Since I was very young, Mom tried to instill a thought in me that without her raising me so tough and well, I would have grown to be some kind of a freak, a bully. I think it was her way to try to justify all the strict behavior she directed at me.

I know many skaters and people in general experience some form of tension among family members, and that's why I feel called to talk openly about my family and the not-always-so-smooth relationship with my dear Mom.

"You don't know what's best for you, I know," "You can't think like that," "You can't feel like that"—these are all sentences Mom would use sometimes in conversations. And oh boy, did she mean what she said. It didn't matter if I tried to explain that that was how I actually felt. If she thought my feeling was not correct for some reason, it did not exist. Back then I obviously didn't realize how harmful and intrusive this kind of behavior is. How internally suffocating it is when you're not allowed to think your own thoughts or feel your own feelings! As a kid, though, I bought into Mom's narrative that there's something inherently wrong with me, and I should be thankful for her for sacrificing so much of herself to parent a wretched person like me.

What has been the most confusing thing about my mom's behavior until now is that one day she could be the most empathetic and caring person in the world and the next day she would attack me, usually mentally or emotionally. Today she might praise me for being such a wonderful daughter and so smart; tomorrow she might blast me for being an ungrateful daughter and somehow "not right" mentally or lacking in empathy.

Only in my adulthood have I started to really come to terms with the fact that my mom's love for me feels sometimes very conditional. If I do everything I possibly can to try to please her and follow her directions, I receive her love and approval. But no matter how much I have tried to please her and do everything according to her will, it has never been good enough, at least not for long. There's always something that I could have done better or differently. It feels utterly exhausting and devastating.

If I voice my own opinion and do as I feel right regardless of her opposing view, it is likely that she would try to guilt me into her control. When as an adult I've tried to discuss with her my feelings of being controlled by her, she goes into complete denial and can't grasp at all what I'm talking about. It's as if we live in different universes. What for me feels like agonizing control feels like love for her. After all, in her mind she only wants the best for me.

Anyway, I was still in elementary school when Dad started to come home drunk. The fights between Mom and Dad became more frequent; the majority of them had to do with his drinking, which in retrospect I think was a result of dysfunctional dynamics in his life and our home. Perhaps it was my dad's desperate way to try to manage. Mom didn't hesitate to vocalize quite loudly even in the middle of the night when Dad would wobble home after a loss. Petra knew that Dad always went to a local pub called Jäähovi on those nights. Sometimes Petra would sneak over to Jäähovi to coax him to come home so that another loud argument might be avoided. Petra always tried so hard to head off unpleasant situations and maintain harmony in our family. That shouldn't be the job of children.

Petra and I prayed that Tappara would win, if only for the sake of peace in our household. Sometimes the fights got so out of control that they were absolutely inappropriate for children to witness. All the aggression, physical, emotional and verbal, and hyper-control at home eventually made me numb to all kinds of pain—one of my coping mechanisms. Later on, the habit of dissociating from pain and numbing my emotions became extreme.

I'm sure that my parents tried their best, but the intense situations forced us to come up with a range of defense mechanisms. For me, at least, these defenses, no matter how adaptive at the time, later became unhealthy habits that were hard to unlearn. Petra and I tried to be extra good so that we wouldn't be an additional "burden" for Mom. During the intense conflicts, we often took Dad's side, maybe because we sensed he suffered at least as much from Mom's overbearing control as she did from his drinking.

There were times when a split was imminent. Our parents never tried to hide those "conversations." Sometimes Petra and I have wondered that maybe it would have been better if Mom and Dad had had the guts to get divorced. Fortunately, Dad understood he had to get help for his drinking problem and started going to AA. He hasn't had a drop in over a decade, and against the odds, the Korpi marriage lives on.

Kiira Korpi

When I think about my parents today, I feel mostly gratitude and love toward them. I wouldn't be where I am today without my family and all those beautiful and tough experiences. Mom, Dad and Petra have taught and continue to teach me so much about life and myself. I'm sure both of my parents have done their very best and loved me and Petra as well as they knew how. Mom and Dad are very dear to me despite all their imperfections, and maybe even because of them.

My family (from left, Mom, me, Petra, and Dad) in Italy on Dad's 60th, 2017.

4

When Everything
Was Still Fun

That girl will be a world-class skater one day. She is so strong-willed, persistent and original.

My first coach Anne described me with these three adjectives, none of which have anything to do with my skating skills or physical attributes. It's a fact. I wasn't able to do much on the ice at first, but the desire to learn was enormous, and I could take in a lot of information quickly. The hardheaded spirit that had been so frustrating for my parents was my greatest gift in figure skating. If I botched a jump, I stood right back up and went into it again even faster, my little bob haircut swinging. I'd wipe out, get up, sore butt and all, and do it again. And so it would go, over and over and over—until I finally managed to land the jump. A good example of my persistence was the fact that I managed to land a double axel for the first time when I was ten. This jump is a rite of passage in skating because you do two and a half rotations in the air, nearly the three revolutions that are required for the magical triple jump.

The practice session is almost over today, and the Zamboni is already gliding out on the ice. Time to wrap up?

I'll try one more time.

A fall.

I have to try one more, just one more.

A fall.

This is the last try. I swear.

...and a successful double axel landed on the backward outside edge. Yes!

I circled the rink again and again. That "fight until you make it" attitude characterized almost my whole competitive career.

Kiira Korpi

My desire to skate burned inside of me from the youngest age. When I was four, Mom gave in to my daily begging and signed me up for the skating school in another town. The club's policy was to only accept kids five and over, but Mom talked them into letting me be with my sister in class. This was January 1993. That was the year we were in Turku, the year of the gold tap. Turku and Tampere in Finland are kind of like Los Angeles and New York City in the States or Rome and Milan in Italy; people feud over which one is better. As strongly as I've been identified with my home city Tampere and my home club Tappara—and I've proudly represented them—I have to confess that my skating life began in Turku.

The skating club's spring show, my first performance ever, was a bit too demanding on my very short patience. I had my butterfly outfit on and was ready to go. Who came up with the boring idea that I had to sit still and wait my turn? The rink was packed because the star of the show was Ronn Moss, aka Ridge Forrester. *The Bold and the Beautiful* was hugely popular in Finland and one million people, one-fifth of the whole country, watched it on TV every day. When Moss came out to greet the audience, there was one little butterfly who decided to choreograph her own move to center stage and fly right alongside him.

Petra (right) and me in our first skating performance in Turku, 1993.

28

4. When Everything Was Still Fun

The following fall Petra and I continued our skating lessons in Klagenfurt, Austria, where my dad was now coaching the hockey team KAC. There was a lady who ran a "skating school," which was essentially a space behind the hockey goal that she used during public skating sessions. Although the rink was always crowded and the figure skating area only a few feet wide, I was overjoyed to get on the ice once a week. I was six years old when we returned home from Austria, and I could now skate at Tappara. I went to a few piano lessons and tried some gymnastics but at the age of six I had found my passion. I did it all the time.

The beginning of my competitive career wasn't promising. I was in last place in my first competition in Tampere, and Petra was second to last. Not exactly a jackpot for the Korpi family. My mother, an elementary school teacher, read us a children's book where Enni Bear organizes a consolation party for Onni Bear when he comes in last in a skiing contest. Mom was especially proud that Petra had had the courage to perform solo, and I was in first place if you turned the scoresheet upside down. At our party we celebrated the upside-down "double victory" of the Korpi sisters. That turned out to be the only party for my skating that was ever held at home.

Petra was more athletic than me and in the beginning was much more skilled at skating. But she lacked the iron will to win. Right from the beginning I had an irresistible drive to learn, and I so wanted to *win*. Petra's character was softer and then there was the fact that she was shy in front of a crowd. Not me! When we performed as kids during the breaks at Tappara hockey games, I crossed my fingers so that the announcer would remember to call out my name and get the crowd to watch me. Petra on the other hand was hoping that when it was her turn to perform, everyone would have already left their seats to buy some of the tasty local sausage. Petra was good, though, and practiced for years, but decided to stop skating after she got injured at 16. After that she tried synchronized skating. This as a team sport and fit her character better than solo skating, but because the level of the team wasn't very high at that time, she decided to focus on her university studies.

After a stint with my first trainer Anne, I moved on to Maaret Siromaa's (Maare's) group in Tappara when I was eight. I was already training about six times a week. Like Anne, my second coach Maare was quick to spot the enthusiasm and speed I had on the ice. She wanted me to skate to Nikolai Rimsky-Korsakov's famous "Flight of the Bumblebee." The fast-paced and sassy composition that lasts just over a minute dramatizes the constantly changing path of the bumblebee. To the audience the spins and circles of the speedy, fluffy bee may have looked reckless and unpredictable. But somehow, she always found her way to her destination and never crashed into anything. At least not very often.

My daring on the ice gave Maare moments of true fear. I didn't always have the patience to stand rinkside and listen to her careful lectures on jump basics. As soon as I felt I had the idea I'd make a break for it at full speed trying my jumps. You can get hurt very badly if you don't know what you're doing, but luckily, I survived with only a few bruises.

Maaret "Maare" Siromaa is one of the icons of Finnish figure skating coaching. She was a professional coach for more than 40 years, and in that time, she coached "almost everyone" in the Finnish skating world. Maare's passion for the sport also unfortunately burned her out a few times over the decades. But she always rolled up her sleeves and got back to work after her breaks. She simply loved coaching and relished the daily grind of teaching dozens of kids under the gloomy lights of the Hakametsä ice rink. Maare continued to work as head coach of Tappara until late 2019 when she decided to retire.

Maare, Maare, Maare. Just saying her name aloud brings on a soft and warm feeling. That's how Maare is, just a wonderful person. As coach and coachee we spent a total of 17 years together. She became a second mother to me, on and off the ice, and we traveled the world to my competitions. She went over my schoolwork with me on flights, shopped at countless pharmacies, reading the labels on flu and cold medicine so I wouldn't accidentally take anything that was banned. She would go out with me super early in the morning to buy fresh fruits and vegetables if the hotel didn't serve them. We were inseparable, especially when I was young and not always accompanied by my parents. At the world junior championships 2004 in the Hague, Valtter Virtanen's coach Liivo Rennik had organized a sightseeing tour for us in the city. Liivo always liked to drag us along to see the tourist sights, not something I always looked forward to.

"Do I have to go sightseeing?" I whispered to Maare.

"Yes. You do. It is important that you learn the culture, history and art of different cities. You need to be trained in that way, too."

As a coach Maare was methodical, but only as I got older did my training become highly systematic and well sequenced. In those early years, I don't remember doing a proper off-ice warm-up before entering the rink. We just kind of warmed up directly on the ice. Nowadays that would be very unusual. We worked hard but with a relaxed and cheerful attitude. Maare believed that was crucial. I remember how much fun we had in training. That was a big reason why I fell in love with figure skating and didn't even want to try any other sport. I never voluntarily missed a training, ever.

> Kiira always wanted to do things just right. Training was precise and Kiira was willing to work very hard. She has refined her steps and edges to perfection! Is that perfectionism or what you call it? I don't know. But that's how Kiira was.—Maaret Siromaa, coach, 1996–2013

Maare was absolutely instrumental in getting my early career going with the Finnish figure skating federation. In 1999, with her encouragement, I applied and was accepted into a training group called "Project 2000." I was 10 going on 11. At the selection trials I scored the maximum on the exam that measured mental resilience. The most promising skaters were chosen for this group, including Laura Lepistö from Espoo, who was born the same year as I was. We immediately got along and had so many things to share. We had a carefree attitude about skating, we loved to goof around and laugh, but we worked super hard in practice. Laura was almost a head shorter than me, a cute little girl. We were a funny looking pair at competitions and camp trips. Back then we couldn't have imagined the adventure we were about to embark on or our intense and rewarding rivalry. Over the next 13 years we traveled to many of the same competitions and won seven championship medals combined.

Laura had been accepted to the federation's training group on her first try, a year before me. I had also been recommended to the group. According to the feedback, I had speed, but I needed dance training. My biggest shortcoming was my jump technique. One of my legs was always bent at the knee as I flew up. This didn't fit the aesthetics of the sport and also affected the clean rotation needed for good jumps. Maare was trying hard to fix that flaw, but I think that I had missed most of her advice while hopping on the ice like a grasshopper. High and fast, never worrying about style. By some miracle, during my first year with Project 2000, Maare helped me clean up my leg position and in March 2000 I won the Finnish championship, juvenile division. It was an under–13 event, and I was 11. Mom, along with Petra, had always thought skating was just a nice hobby for me, but when I won that event, it made them reconsider.

Kiira Korpi

When Kiira won the Finnish juvenile championship, being younger than most contestants, the win felt good. It was a win for the whole club, not only for Kiira, because Tappara figure skating had been a laughingstock in the early years. That's when I first realized that Kiira is very talented.—Brita Korpi, mother

Regardless, according to Mom, she *still* thought of my skating as basically a hobby, even though I'd already been training for years. Mom says she didn't act like she had a top athlete living at home but a schoolgirl. I can't say I completely agree with this notion. I feel that skating influenced so much of our whole family's life from the time I was young.

I never went to see the practice or demanded anything from the coaches. In general, I never talked about Kiira's skating, very rarely I would talk about skating at all.—Brita Korpi, mother

The win at the Finnish championships meant I would get to take my first trip abroad. I was slated to go to Zagreb with the Project 2000 group. We were led by head coach Pirjo "Piitu" Uimonen. Coach Piitu reminded we first-time travelers to drink enough water, stay hydrated! OK, people? Another member of the team was Christina Wendelin from Koovee, Tampere. "Kyrsse" and I decided that our hydration would consist of drinking as much 7UP as possible. We drank loads of it in our hotel room and giggled so much it spewed from our noses. I debuted my international competition career under the effects of a big sugar rush, swollen feet, and a lemony, bubbly tummy. I came in second.

Thinking back to my early career, I have fond memories of the summer training camps. Those were the best times and I saw some incredible places in the world. Tartu, Lake Arrowhead in California, Vierumäki, Flims. What could be better than spending time with friends in the summer and training together? There was a warm sense of community. It was also an opportunity to get to know foreign skaters and later to have an eye out for the boys.

At times we had weird ideas. In midsummer at the Tartu camp our apartment was like a bad sauna. My teammate Niina Laksola and I decided to cool off by rubbing ice gel all over our bodies and wrapping ourselves in wet towels. In Vierumäki, Niina and I, dared by AP, sneaked into a closed diving tower and took a ten-meter drop into Lake Valkjärvi. I belly flopped into the water and got the wind knocked out of me. AP had promised us ice cream if we did it. (This was Ari-Pekka

Eleven years old in Croatia, the Mladost Trophy in 2000, my first inter-national competition and medal. From left: me (silver medal) Aki Sawada from Japan (gold), Eri Ishigami from Japan (bronze), and Christina Wen-delin (fourth place). The others skaters are unidentified.

Nurmenkari, one of the best Finnish male figure skaters, tall and about five years older than me, not to mention Finnish national champion seven times. I guess you don't say no to AP.) At one point, we had the annoying habit of transforming our voices into a strange whimper, which must have been highly annoying to the adults in our life. Our parents probably were close to nervous breakdowns as we continued rehearsing that whiny tone at home.

Training buddies were very important for me in my junior years. We had a good community at Tappara. In addition to Niina, our group consisted of Maria Tupala, Salla Hankivuo, and Krista Suhonen, among others. Krista was the most talented one among us, but she wasn't as hardworking at practice. She won the Finnish junior championships but never broke into the top rankings as an adult. Niina and I became very close friends. I joined her and her family on a skiing holiday in Lapland and we spent a lot of time together outside training. Once Niina and I tried to get into an establishment that didn't allow underage patrons. It didn't cross our minds that I was already well known in the media.

Petra's ID wasn't very effective, and we didn't make it past the doors of Bar Passion.

At the training camps I shared a room with Niina and after practice we'd watch Tappara or Ilves. We were both big fans. Niina's dad was national team player Reijo Laksola and had been in the '76 Olympics. In Finland, he played for Ilves. And her mom was a fantastic Olympic skier, Riitta Ollikka-Laksola. Niina won the Nordic championships gold medal in 2006. Then, her dad, a person beloved across Finland, passed away suddenly in 2007. Among my training friends she was the one who continued skating the longest. However, when we reached our 20s, all my friends from Tappara had stopped skating, including Niina. I stayed in the club for years without my first friends. The so-called locker room life was over and attending practice felt like going to work, but without work buddies. When I stood by the rink watching hockey, I would sometimes wish I was involved in team sports.

> Kiira had exceptional focus; I have never seen anything like it. When Kiira, for example, read a book in a car she needed to be called to almost ten times if you wanted an answer.—Niina Laksola, childhood and skating friend

In 2001 I moved to the novice level in under–16 competitions. At 12 years of age I was the youngest competitor in the Finnish championship, and I finished fifth. The following year I won the Finnish championship in the same category and won an international novice competition held in Dortmund, Germany. I practiced 11 times a week and by this point I had learned all the triple jumps, which was key.

In figure skating, people talk about a first phase of intensive learning which continues until you're about 12. During that phase all the difficult tricks should be learned in order to ensure their complete integration into the athletic skill set. Sure, difficult jumps can be mastered and integrated later on as well, but it becomes much more difficult after a certain age. During puberty, changes to the body and mind kick in. It's no wonder that in recent years there are ever-younger skating virtuosos, especially from Russia. Without the age restrictions, we would see even younger skaters at major competitions.

My development accelerated rapidly after I got into Project 2000. I improved even more in the International Skating Union's development program, which sponsored Nordic coach-athlete duos. Maare and I worked hard, but at that time I wasn't especially skilled or the most talented skater of the group. Much later, when I was filming a movie about the skating legend Sonja Henie in the summer of 2017, one Norwegian skating coach told me she remembered me well from the ISU camps. She told me that they had a saying in their club that every skater might have a Kiira Korpi in them. What she meant by this was that anyone can succeed by working hard even if the prospects don't look so good in the beginning. It felt amazing to hear that.

The ISU development group got together regularly in Vierumäki where top coaches such as Frank Carroll, Aleksei Mishin, Viktor Kudriavtsev, Kathy Casey, Don Laws, and Anne Shelter were invited to help out. Coach Shelter held skating skill workshops that were known as "Annie's Edges." Anne's work meant so much to me. In recent years I've had the chance to work with skater-coach duos, and it feels wonderful to now be the one offering inspiration and encouragement.

> Kiira lifted the spirit at practices and camps with her natural positivity. She is so super positive. If for some reason Kiira was absent from a practice the whole atmosphere was missing something.—Anuliisa Uotila, figure skating coach and national team head coach, 2002–2012

In 2002, Susanna Haarala joined our team at Tappara. I was excited about it: in Helsinki, Susanna had coached Elina Kettunen. With Susanna at her side, Elina had placed fifth in the European championships and 11th in world championship and Olympic rankings. I knew that Susanna was a tough coach but also that she was just the right match for me at that moment. I was happy about the composition of our team, with Susanna and Maare complementing each other well.

> When I moved to Tappara, there was talk of Kiira being a young and very promising skater, but I didn't know her at all at that time. I noticed that Kiira was a sporty girl, a strong jumper. She was athletic but still rough around the edges. Stiff and awkward when performing.—Susanna Haarala, Kiira's coach, 2002–2013

Susanna had graduated with a master's in sport and health sciences from Jyväskylä University and she had a sports instructor degree from Vierumäki. During her college years she was already taken on as an assistant to the Estonian coach Tiiu Valgemäki. She was known for applying cutting-edge theory, especially when it came to physical training. Susanna has a commanding knowledge of physiology. Through Elina, she had the fresh experience of international operations and developed some strong views on how training should be done. Right from the start Susanna increased the number of my training sessions and we now included three early morning sessions per week.

Another thing about Susanna was her ambition and a kind of stubbornness, both a strength and weakness. In this way, Susanna and I were very similar. She demanded top-notch work from her athletes at each training session. Petra and the other skaters at the club who had never practiced in such a goal-oriented way were even afraid of Susanna. They didn't want a coach after them all the time, demanding more and more, sometimes shouting across the ice. Susanna coached everyone like they had to become top athletes—now! Maare, on the other hand, could adjust better to the skater. In the locker room we would be nervously guessing which of the coaches we'd have that day—Maare or Susanna. If it was Maare, there'd be a big breath of relief. Maare and Susanna were like night and day, but for me the ensemble worked. They complemented each other perfectly, all the better for our team.

Susanna lifted training to a completely new level. I don't think I would have developed into such a strong figure skater without Susanna. She had a fire in the belly for coaching, so much that sometimes it erupted as frustration. Sometimes she'd even get anxious during warm-ups if my moves weren't clean enough. We discovered that Susanna would be in an especially demanding mood when she got back from international competitions or camps. She would compare our skills to those of top skaters and was frustrated when we couldn't get close to that level.

The roles and dynamics of our coaching team became well established, and it all started to fit together. I tended to think positively, as did Maare. Susanna was harshly realistic and would pull the carpet out from under our feet if we had pie in the sky expectations. Susanna would observe my trainings super closely. If in her opinion we didn't have a strong run of practices, she wouldn't have high hopes for my upcoming performances. If she felt the training was going well, her expectations were through the roof. That's what happened at the Bern European championships in January 2011. I was in top shape and led the competition after the short program.

Figure skating competitions always include two segments: the short program and the free program, which are skated on consecutive days. The short program includes seven mandatory technical elements while the free program has 12. In the total score, the free program has much more weight, and after I skated one of my worst free programs of the season in Bern, I dropped to bronze. During the medal party organized by the federation, Maare had to practically *order* Susanna to smile because it was so obvious that she was massively disappointed. Susanna expected great things when I had what it took. This had been one of those times.

After Susanna joined the team, it showed in my results. At 14, I moved up to the junior level, which is officially from the age of 13 to 19 for young women. During the next two seasons I won the Nordic championship in the juniors twice (2003 and 2004) and Finnish championship in the juniors (2004). I earned Finnish championship silver in the juniors (2003) finishing second after Laura Lepistö. However, as the Nordic champion, I was chosen over Laura as Finland's sole representative in the junior world championships in Ostrava, Czech Republic, in 2003. I was the youngest skater in the competition.

The experienced Finnish judge Hely Abbondati sat in the middle of the judge's panel. The International Skating Union had named her the referee of the junior world championships. The referee heads the panel of judges and may also serve as a judge herself. Back then the JWC included a qualification round before the short program, and in that round, I jumped a clean triple Lutz for the first time in a competition. Hely, much respected in the International Skating Union, suddenly jumped out of her seat.

"Wow! The Finnish skater did a triple Lutz!"

She awkwardly sat right back down, still smiling. I succeeded with the Lutz also in my short program and was 19th overall in my junior world championship debut.

Learning the various jumps in figure skating can add to the enjoyment of watching the sport and I want to share that with you. The Lutz is the most difficult of the six jumps of the sport and it also generates the most points—that's why Hely got so excited about it. The Lutz, like the toe loop and flip, are so-called toe jumps that take off backward by using the sharp toe pick. The loop and Salchow also take off backward but straight from the edge of the blade without the help of the toe pick kick. The Axel is the easiest jump to recognize because it's the only one that takes off forward.

I competed in the junior world championships three times, with my best finish being tenth in Kitchener, Ontario, in 2005. Maare and Susanna wanted me to go for four in a row. They thought it would have been good for me to compete under pressure and with a good chance of medaling. I was still in the age category but then I unexpectedly qualified for something very special and so I never did a fourth juniors. I was headed to the Torino Olympics in 2006! After that almost everyone in Finland knew who Kiira Korpi was.

The Ice and Me

The pressure on the edge feels just right. I don't press down on the ice too strongly. I feel energy going upward through my body. My skates glide on the ice softly and respond to my directions without effort. I feel the center line of my body, and each move feels elastic in every direction. I feel soft, flexible and explosive all at once.

Thoughts pass through my mind like clouds in a blue sky. They come and go, but I don't get stuck on them, because I am so strong inside. Some odd thoughts appear, but I let them float away. I can't lose this strength. I send a message of freedom and relaxation to my body by breathing deeply, keeping my chest open and smiling softly. I don't give in to my nerves and I allow my posture to rise and energy to bloom.

The movements begin deep inside my spine and the music gives me more power. When I'm spinning, I can feel the centrifugal force wiping away any lingering insecurity, and when I'm taking off to jump, I already know how I will meet the ice again on a perfect backward outside edge as I land. The movements merge into each other seamlessly, nothing feels forced or disconnected. I don't need to push or pull, just enjoy the sense of weightlessness.

⇒ 5 ⇐

Olympic-Size Nerves

The bus pulled into the parking lot. Even if it was out of sight, we could *feel* the glow of the Olympic torch as evening was darkening.

"Hi. Can we help you in any way? Carry your bags to housing, maybe?"

Was this Saku Koivu speaking to me? To me?! Or maybe to Maare, but anyway, wow. And Teemu Selänne knew my name! My 40-something coach and I were giggling while two hulking NHL stars lifted our luggage out of the bus cargo hold. Saku was on the Montreal Canadiens, and Teemu played for the Anaheim Mighty Ducks. Teemu was known as the "Finnish Flash" and became the highest-scoring Finn in NHL history, not to mention the 16th all-time scorer. Wow. A few weeks earlier I had been in high school preparing for my prom with my friends, and now I was hanging out with Saku Koivu and Teemu Selänne at the Olympics.

I wasn't meant to be at the Olympics. I had thought maybe Vancouver in 2010. I was only 17 years old in Torino. How did this magical thing happen?

My road to the Olympics started a year earlier in Oulu, Finland. In December of 2004, I was competing in the adult Finnish championships for the first time. After my big success in the juniors, my aim was to get at least fourth place, maybe even snag a medal if I could keep my programs solid. To get to the top three meant that I needed to outdo at least one of the more accomplished skaters like Susanna Pöykiö, Alisa Drei or Elina Kettunen. They were all favorites for medaling. Alisa had won gold in two previous Finnish championships, Ellu (Elina) had been fifth in the European championships a few seasons earlier, and Sussu (Susanna) had made it to the top ten at the European level three times. When I think about Finnish female skaters, past and present, Sussu's skating style is the one I admire most. So soft, elegant, and silent—simply beautiful.

Six years older than me, Sussu had been my idol for such a long time. I looked up to Elina and Alisa, too. It felt wonderful to get to compete against them.

Ellu skated an unsuccessful short program in Oulu, and before the free program, I was in third place after Sussu and Alisa. My chance for a medal became a reality when Alisa got sick with the stomach flu and had to withdraw. In the free skating portion, I got the best technical score in the whole competition and made silver in the Finnish championships, right behind Sussu! Finland had three spots for the January 2005 European championships. Suddenly, at the age of 16, I was on the EC team.

There was some controversy about who should be in the third spot. The choice was between Ellu and Alisa. When Ellu was chosen, Alisa flung her skates out of the hotel window. At least that was the rumor. Peter Pomoell, the vice chairman of the federation at the time, said that Ellu had a better personal record that season than Alisa. OK, but no one had been informed they would be picking the European championship team like that. After intense public criticism, the federation agreed that its criteria for rankings and team choices needed to be more clearly spelled out.

The 2005 European championships were held in the Palavela arena in Torino. I was in a good situation. Because I was a young first-timer, there wasn't a lot of pressure on me.

> If Korpi reaches the top 24 of the 37 skaters in the short program and joins the free skating program—that would be a great achievement for this super promising skater.—*Kaleva*, January 28, 2005

Sussu's situation was tougher. Finland was waiting for our first medal for a female skater at the European championships. All eyes were on her. That year she was the fifth best European in the world rankings. Sussu had won bronze in the junior world championships in 2001, and this European championship was seen as her best shot, maybe one of her last. Sussu and Ellu had been knocking on the door of the top three since the early 2000s, but a medal for Finland was still missing.

I was more nervous for Sussu than I was for myself. We all waited and watched with our hearts beating for her. Then she did it! She skated to European silver, second only to Russian skater Irina Slutskaya. This was an historical achievement. Her win was a huge inspiration for me. I had renewed faith that Finnish skaters could succeed in international championships. One major element in the mix was the new scoring system. It was launched at the European championships. The new system reformed the biased judging practices that made it difficult for people from smaller countries to medal. With the old 6.0 system the power of major skating countries unfortunately often showed in the results, which could be predicted by looking at the skaters' nationalities. With the new system, the power of individual judges was thankfully diluted.

The new system contained many good reforms. Finnish coaches and skaters adapted to them more quickly than many other countries did. In the old system, a spin could be spun almost any which way, but now it became important to follow the exact guidelines for each spin and think about the exact position of your body as it rotates. Also, every turn and move of the mandatory step sequence counts. The transitions between elements needed to be fluid but precise. Of all the countries, I think only Canada took to the new judging criteria as quickly as we did.

Ellu finished 11th in the competition. I was in 13th place at my European championship debut. It was the first of eight European championships of my career, and the only one where I didn't finish in the top six.

Ellu's career suddenly came to an end in the fall of 2005, which smoothed my path to the Finnish championship medals in the next season. In December 2005 I made bronze in the Finnish championships in my home arena Hakametsä. The whole medal trio, Sussu, Alisa and I, were selected to go to the European championships in Lyon in spring 2006. The name of the game was clear: the two best Finns in that competition would then get to go to the Torino Olympics, only a month later.

All season long I tried not to think about the Olympics, although reporters would ask me about them every now and then. My team figured that after the European championships I would go on to the junior world championships and fight for a medal there. This was a very reasonable plan and so when I went to the 2006 European championships I could compete without crazy pressure. This was not the case for other Finnish skaters, especially Alisa. Alisa was ten years older than me and had already been to the Nagano Olympics in 1998. The competition in Lyon was just about her last chance to get to the Olympics again. For me, on the other hand, there were still many chances. In Vancouver in 2010, I would be only 21 years old, and if I qualified for Sochi 2014, I'd still be in my 20s. My only aim at the EC was to finish in the top ten. But then...

Kiira Korpi

Torino is calling! Kiira Korpi surprisingly arose as the best Finn at the figure skating European Championships.—*Ilta-Sanomat*, January 20, 2006

Like so many other times, I did excellently when I got to skate without pressure and huge expectations. I was still behind Sussu and Alisa after the short program, but my free skate was good enough to help me climb to sixth place, and when the dust cleared, I was the best Finn at the European championships! Sussu was seventh and Alisa eighth, and we all placed within five points of each other.

Long story short, the two skaters selected to go to the Olympics were Sussu—and me! I had made it by the thinnest margin. The point difference was so small that one failed jump might have changed everything, but that free program performance set the course for the rest of my career.

Kiira Korpi is an Olympic princess.—*Ilta-Sanomat*, February 18, 2006

The fans can't keep up. Korpi turns everyone's head.—*Aamulehti*, February 3, 2006

I can't say I didn't dream of this moment, but I had not dared to think it could really happen. Now that it was a reality, I was thrown off my feet. I had not prepared for this situation at all. It was all new for my coaches, too, mostly because they never coached someone of my age and inexperience in this situation.

Susanna had been in the Salt Lake City Olympics with Ellu four years prior, but according to Susanna, Ellu had been completely ready to compete at the Olympic level. I had never even been to the world championships. I believed that my technique wasn't strong enough to make a strong showing at Torino, but I had a core of belief in myself, under all the stormy feelings. I often managed to pull off a miracle but, seriously, my coaches were worried. I was a fierce competitor, but maybe I put too much faith in my ability to "come from behind." Still, underneath all the doubts was pure desire—I wanted so much to be there, to skate. In those days, I was often able to set aside the worries and inner voices and connect with my strength.

There was only a month between the European championships and the Olympics, and we were in a rush to figure out all the practical issues. I was still in high school, and it was exam time, but in order to get ready for the Olympics, I had to skip a few! I missed my prom, too. My date Eero fortunately paired up with an older girl. This was lucky because in Finland you had to dance traditional folk dances and waltzes, and it takes months of practice before a couple is ready. I was relieved that now he wouldn't be left in the lurch after all our preparation together.

Now the publicity was really getting out of control. To add to all the pressure, I had to upgrade my skating programs, which had to feature more difficult sequences and jumps. For the first time, we added the very challenging triple-triple combinations. Then, right before we left, I came down with a cold. When we got to Torino, I still had a little cough.

After Saku and Teemu's warm welcome by the bus, I was given directions to my room, my *solo* room. Initially I was supposed to stay with Sussu, but we had to be sure I wasn't contagious. Sussu told me to stay away from her. I was handed my key and told my lodging was somewhere at the edge of the Olympic village. I wandered along the dark lanes by myself looking for the place. The flat was completely unfinished, as were a lot of other things at the village. I plopped down my bags. OK, well, here I am, now what?

In those first few hours I felt miserable and alone, cut off from the rest of the Finnish team. Teenage moodiness? It all passed. Within a day, I was among my teammates, feeling very welcome and cozy. But my inner anxiety continued, and that showed in my early results.

> Korpi almost didn't make the cut. The failed triple-triple combination cost points in the short program.—*Aamulehti*, February 22, 2006

A short program requires three jump elements, one of which is a jump combination. In a combination, jumps are done in sequence; the skater takes off for the second jump directly after landing the first. Combinations are the most point-rich elements and often start off a program when you have enough strength to do two triple jumps one after the other. When I was only 15 seconds into my program my combination jumps ended up as doubles instead of triples. This mistake cost me a lot of points. Overwhelmed by disappointment I made a face and shrugged briefly when I finished my program. The cameras caught it, but I think the person making the biggest deal about it was Tarja. Team captain Tarja Ristanen wasn't too happy about my negative body language, which is considered very poor etiquette in our sport. According to Tarja it was unwise to express negative emotions in front of the judges, especially right at the end of a program.

I don't know what I think about this unwritten rule. In figure skating you're supposed to skate with style no matter what mistakes you make, and at the end, graciously thank the audience and smile. I get that. A ballerina never shows her disappointment while she's exiting the stage, does she? But wouldn't showing a wider range of emotion on the ice make the sport a little more human? Figure skaters are not machines, but athletes who, just like those in any other sport, feel joy and disappointment. Appearances at championship competitions are the result of years of hard work. I think it's weird to not express our feelings at these make-or-break events. I don't know if my antics dragged down my score, but after the short program, I was 20th, barely qualifying for the group of 24 who would skate the free program.

> Kiira loved competing even though it made her nervous and scared. As the underdog or challenger Kiira always did better; it was easier for her mentally. The times when Kiira was leading the competition after a short program were more difficult situations for her.—Maaret Siromaa, Kiira's coach, 1996–2013

Throughout my whole competitive career I would get horrible nerves. In Torino, the worst nerves hit me on the morning of the free program. This was weird, as one might think my Olympic debut in the short program would have been the scariest bit.

With me the nervousness takes over so much that on mornings like that I start asking myself why I even skate. Why do I put myself into that uncomfortable situation again and again? My stomach reacts strongly to nerves, and in my worst moments I needed anti-diarrhea medicine before heading out there. Imagine how it feels when, during a six-minute warm-up, you have to, on top of everything else, wonder if you can hold it! I've heard that anti-diarrhea medicine is pretty popular at the Olympics.

Those competition nerves would start creeping up on me in my home arena during my last few practices before a competition. I tried lots of things. I would force myself to run through my programs straight through, imagining it was the day of the competition. But that would make those final practices unfocused. Mentally I had thrown myself into the future, but my body was still at the practice rink. A lot of athletes I know have had the same feeling of being separated from their bodies when their minds start to race and anticipate too much. I also tried to ease my nerves by doing visualization training and relaxation exercises, trying to imagine a successful performance. These exercises would help briefly.

5. Olympic-Size Nerves

In one interview I did when I was 13, I boldly said that competitions never make me nervous. The reality is that I have always felt nervous before a competition, but at 13 I still had a child-like confidence in my ability to always perform well. I was not yet overwhelmed by all the pressures that build up when you're a year-round performer, not to mention that at 13 I could never imagine the intense media attention I would get around the time of my first Olympics.

In Torino, there was a whole day between the short program and the free program, a much longer gap than I was used to. Typically, the free program is the day after the short program. Time was crawling—the worst thing about being nervous was the wait. When the day arrived, at 6 a.m., we were already out there. That was torturous because after practice there were many long hours before the competition in the evening. I tried to rest, I did my hair and makeup routine, but I was still so jittery. Just seeing the five Olympic rings put a pit in my stomach. It was all too real: This is it! Four minutes all alone on the ice while millions are watching! Before the free program that evening I went to eat in the cafeteria at the Olympic village. There I ran into the ice hockey players from the national team.

"How are you feeling, Kiira?" Teppo Numminen asked.

"I'm so nervous," I answered, eyes staring wide.

"It's going to go well. Just do as you would in a training session."

There wasn't much time left when Teppo gave me that spirit talk. His words went beyond coaching clichés to a whole spirit of courage, a spirit of feeling part of something bigger than myself. Nothing like that had ever happened to me at a competition and I'll remember his words forever. I felt the rush of being part of the Finnish team. That energy worked on me and in me, right through my free program.

Korpi celebrated, Pöykiö was disappointed.—*Iltalehti*, February 24, 2006

I still didn't make the triple-triple combination, but I finished in 16th place overall, while Sussu finished 13th. The stated goal of our Olympic team was achieved, a top–16 finish. I was awarded a Sisu-knife, the symbolic gift for a good performance for a Finnish athlete.*

---

* The Sisu is a legendary knife awarded to athletes by the Finnish Olympic Committee. Sisu in Finnish means determination/perseverance. After 9/11 you couldn't travel with a knife on an airplane; that's why the FOC eventually stopped awarding physical Sisu knives. But in 2006 I got a real knife. I still have it!

Kiira Korpi

Kiira was one of the people who lit up a spark for me. When I saw Kiira skate in the Torino Olympics I got a great passion to show what I can do. That escalated my development. I saw that Kiira did everything on point: nutrition, muscle care, recovery. I realized that I should probably also take sports more seriously.—Laura Lepistö

After my own competition I got to watch Tanja Poutiainen ski to silver as well as the Finnish ice hockey team's Olympic final.

Tarja Halonen, the president of Finland at the time, offered me and Maare a lift to watch another event. I was stressed out about how to speak formally with her. The anxiety evaporated when Tarja turned out to be super laid back. We both changed out of our winter clothes in the bathroom on the way from the ski stadium to the curling matches. I met Tarja several other times, too. The following year she invited me to the President's Independence Day Reception.

Compared to the explosion of fame and pressure that was to come, my Torino experience was relatively carefree, especially after the incredibly supportive words of Teppo and the way the whole team emanated a feeling of togetherness, support, and good spirits. But the tidal wave

Finnish president Halonen and I at the 2006 Olympics.

46

of expectations was starting to hit me, and it was just beginning. I have often thought whether my career would have been different if I hadn't had these early successes. I'm not sure, as these experiences helped me through more difficult times later on. Either way, after Torino, I heard people say that I was a widely admired role model. I don't know about that, but I did need to learn how to watch my words and behavior in public—and I had to do that overnight.

⇒ 6 ⇐

Everyone's Kiira

Even before the Olympics, the publicity was blowing up. One day I was a 16-year-old high school student and the next I'm the so-called "ice princess" of Finland. Interview requests were crashing the doors of the arena. Our ice rink was a public place where anyone could just walk in, take pictures and ask questions—and they did. I was faced with all kinds of distractions. Everything happened so fast that I hadn't gotten a chance to hire a manager. Dad, Mom and Petra tried to help, and so did the coaches, but a lot was on me. My phone number wasn't private, so reporters called me directly.

Dad probably fielded lots of communication he didn't tell me about. He had a little fun turning down some reporters with his standard joke: "You know what, I won't take this suggestion to Kiira but I have an option for you. Tapani Kansa is always up for interviews."

Tapani was a singer in his 70s who had been in the public eye since 1968 and was constantly on TV. Dad pulled this line with dozens of reporters, especially if the reporter seemed insensitive to how much time one interview could take. Even a short shoot or interview trip to Helsinki meant missing at least half a day of training and studying.

To save time, we decided to organize a press event about the upcoming Torino Olympics right there in my local arena, Hakametsä. The dressing room was packed, and even media outlets that had nothing to do with figure skating were there, like *Ruotuväki* (which covered the Finnish military) and a magazine for garlic lovers.

True to my personality, I very much wanted to please people. My calendar was soon completely booked. If I had an hour to spare at some point in the week, I would fill it with an interview. Looking back at the pages of my 2006 planner I am amazed how I managed at all. I didn't know how to look after my own well-being.

My practice routine suffered, and it showed in my results almost immediately. To everyone's surprise I finished outside the top three in the Finnish championships. Susanna Rahkamo, the chairperson of the Finnish figure skating federation at the time, got pretty angry at Maare and Susanna for letting me do all those interviews and shoots. My two coaches had tears in their eyes about the accusations as they tried to explain how hard it was to control the publicity. Maare and Susanna were constantly prioritizing training, but we were *all* so new to this.

During the national team camp I had some training on how to politely answer reporters' questions, but this was not nearly enough. You would think that my local club or at least the Federation would have had a plan to protect young athletes from the combined stress of media attention, training, and schoolwork. But considering how stubborn I was, I don't know if I would have listened to them anyway. I added to the problem by taking the interviews so seriously. I prepared for each one, pondering how I should answer questions in order to keep sponsors, supporters, coaches, and parents happy. I kept thinking, "How is Kiira Korpi, 'ice princess,' role model, etc., etc., going to answer these questions?" This was a danger sign I did not recognize at the time. Already the public and private Kiira were pulling apart.

When I think back now to how things unfolded before, during, and after the Torino Olympics, I realize I was changing in a big way, and not for the better. During the Torino Olympics, it hadn't hit me yet. I was still relatively relaxed and spontaneous in interviews. But then, as I started to strategize, writing out the themes I wanted to stress in my public speech, I was allowing my sense of self to be weakened, fractured. I wasn't creating a fake persona, but the truth was that the tension between the public and private Kiira was starting to tear at me from the inside.

After speaking to reporters I often felt empty and mentally exhausted. Things got better when Mikko Luukkaa joined the team as my manager. I met with Mikko to plan how speak to the media, but I continued to be painfully self-conscious. Did I answer OK? Did I say anything wrong? This is the type of thing I learned from my mom. She read everything I said in the media and got very nervous if something didn't feel right to her. So, in a way, I didn't want to disappoint her. Nor anyone else. Unconsciously I thought I'd be more loved when I did everything "right."

Like a lot of teenagers, I was highly emotional and still growing in so many ways. Nowadays, as a coach and children's rights advocate, I worry about the vulnerability of young people in the public spotlight, and elite figure skaters are getting younger and younger! As for me, I felt that some reporters wanted something from me that I didn't want to give; they wanted to dig too deeply into my personal life. They were way too curious!

> Kiira was very sensitive to all the influences surrounding her. She reacted strongly to her own thoughts as well as everything external. If the sport reporters were present on a given day, I could predict the training would be ruined. At first, I thought that it would be a good chance to train under pressure, but no. Not at all. Kiira was panicking.—Maaret Siromaa, Kiira's coach, 1996–2013

Many journalists were all too focused on my physical appearance and any possible "boyfriends." Early on I took the stance that I would not talk about private matters in my interviews. My decision to avoid conversations about my private life turned out to be wise, even if it didn't hold back the tide, but most journalists did eventually realize that there was no point asking me about my love life or my family. Also, with very few exceptions, I never agreed to do an interview with my dad. Mom worried that I would open myself up to the animosity of anti–Tappara fans if I showed up in the media with Dad. Still, things did not turn out so perfectly.

I proudly believed that I would be able to control the publicity but that's not how it works. I remember that my looks were first brought up in the media during the junior world championships when I was only 15. In 2008, U.S. figure skating reporter Barry Mittan referred to me as "the most beautiful woman in figure skating." That same year, I was the world's 38th most beautiful female face, according to the Annual Independent Critics listing. First on the list was superstar Natalie Portman, and I was ranked as "more beautiful" than Nicole Kidman and Scarlett Johansson. In March 2008 in the *Iltalehti* newspaper poll I was chosen woman of the year and in April the most beautiful woman in Finland. I was first in the Bleacher Report's listing of the sexiest women in sports— see how well I managed to keep the media focused on my skating?!

My concept of an ideal body wasn't based on fashion magazines or Hollywood, certainly not the sexy images the media was trying to build up. Instead, I wanted a body that I thought would be great for figure skating, as muscular and as thin as possible. I was pleased that my breasts were small, and I wished my butt had been smaller, too. I thought I was too tall for a figure skater, and I hoped that I wouldn't grow another inch. I made daily choices about food, hair, nutrition, and fashion with the sport in mind. My obsession with body type led to some problems later on.

I was highly sensitive to public commentary. I stressed about my looks, and there were mixed messages from all sides. Finnish culture emphasizes modesty, and I was influenced by that especially at school, where I tried really hard to blend into the background. If newspaper stories about me were put up on the school's bulletin board among other students' successes, soon my face in the picture was smudged over. I felt sad and tried to figure out a way to hide my success better. On the other hand, the media and skating world were throwing out a lot of demands and expectations. An image of me started to be put out there—a skater that had every ingredient to be a star: looks, sponsors, and already some success on the international championship level. The only trouble was, I didn't feel like a star at all. I was convinced that I should be athletically much stronger in order to deserve all that attention. I was consistent in my messaging on this: I tried to explain over and over that figure skating was not a beauty contest but a serious, strenuous, and highly disciplined sport. I talked a lot about our tough training regimen.

I was trying hard to break up the glittery public image of the "ice princess" because it wasn't true. I mean, it's true that my sport thrives on a sense of magic, and a certain stylish "look" is part of it all. I don't object to that at all, but there's so much more to figure skating than the aesthetics. The sheer strength, discipline, and focus it takes are the result of years of practice. In the early aughts, figure skating audiences, not to mention some sports journalists, did not fully understand the realities of training and preparation, what really went into those performances that looked so effortless on the ice. Maare and Susanna helped a lot by encouraging me to keep the media focused on the athletic and competitive dimensions. My parents were on board as well. But that added pressure, too, and sometimes, even if it wasn't my fault at all, I felt I "failed" an interview if the conversation drifted to my looks or the big question, repeated over and over, of whether I had a boyfriend. One slip and I wouldn't just be failing myself but my coaches and parents, too.

I also felt guilty about the publicity because I knew that many athletes made huge efforts to get sponsor money while I was in a pretty good position—but only after a period of financial stress for my family.

I started to wonder if I was even worth the big expectations and all the attention.

> People thought that I was upset that Kiira was in the headlines much more than I was. Quite the contrary. I would have not wanted to be in Kiira's position. I did later get my sponsors, publicity and Euros for my successes.—Laura Lepistö

I supposedly became a role model for many young people, but I didn't fully understand what that meant. I had my *own* role models growing up. When I was younger, I idolized Susanna Pöykiö and her soft, smooth skating style. When I eventually met her, she welcomed me warmly to the national team and kept me very close. I learned a lot from Sussu, including making nutrition a crucial part of a training regimen. I also admired another wonderful Finnish skater, Alisa Drei. I remember practicing a single movement from a video over and over, so I could learn to do the tango as smoothly as she did. Wow.

But my most worn-out VHS tapes were of Michelle Kwan. I was just in awe at how this five-time world champion made skating look so easy, so flowing. The U.S.-born Kwan also had big stage presence and a magical connection with the music. I hoped and prayed I also possessed this kind of sensitivity. She sang with her body. I met Michelle for the first time the summer before the Torino Olympics at Lake Arrowhead, California. I got to say hi to her and tried to film her practice from the audience. Michelle glanced at me with a grimace and her coach came over to tell me that recording Michelle's programs was not permitted. I was really looking forward to meeting her again in Torino, but she opted out a short time before the Olympics got underway.

I felt a strong sense of responsibility to my younger fans. I remembered how important Sussu and Michelle had been to me. I felt honored. I especially wanted to inspire children to have a healthy, active lifestyle. I felt so happy and humbled when a young woman would shed tears of happiness when meeting me. Being a role model was a burden—because I *made* it a burden. I felt I needed to fit the role of the flawless Finnish maiden that was depicted in the media and by my sponsors, the notion I am always overly optimistic and never hurt anyone's feelings.

Only now after my skating career is over, and as my world has expanded, I realize that people were not as keyed into every single thing I did as much I thought they were. That was a pressure I put on myself, and my team sometimes contributed to the problem. It's better to live the life that you feel is right deep inside. When you are content with yourself, the good energy radiates to the people around you. Today I try to live my life in a way that I don't betray myself and my values, even if it means some people will reject the things I say or do, and even when sometimes my own mind tries to resist my heart's will. Staying real and truthful to myself and others is a daily practice.

> Kiira always wanted to be very positive in the media. I thought the situation would have been easier if Kiira didn't always try to be so very positive. Everything can't always be amazing, sometimes things can be bad as well.—Susanna Haarala, Kiira's coach, 2002–2013

As the publicity grew, the positive feedback grew, too. But I wasn't able to fully appreciate it. The unfortunate thing was that I had a really hard time truly welcoming the thousands of messages of love and appreciation I was given in person, by mail or virtually. Somewhere deep down in my mind I doubted my worth as a human being. I thought if only these people really knew me, they would take those nice words back.

The number of negative comments online proliferated as well. I was already becoming so self-critical, and considering the brain's natural negativity bias, I "heard" this negativity more loudly. There were comments out there that I scored high with judges because of my appearance. But I would also be called ugly or an annoying whiner. My IQ was questioned, and my falls would be listed as my biggest achievements on the ice. Mom was frantic about all that nasty stuff out there. She browsed through online forums and took it all too seriously. Mikko advised her to let it go or she'd be absorbing all that bad energy. Actually, I also peeked into websites and forums, but I grew a thick skin, or so I thought. I was more disappointed if the newspaper headlines were untrue or biased than if some people felt like being nasty that day.

I started to receive mean messages on social media and so did Mikko, sometimes on his phone. Most of the messages were harmless but some were flat out threatening. Mikko contacted the police to ask how to handle situations like that. One man wrote Mikko and said he would get rid of any rivals so that he could marry me. I also got a letter at my house with the return address being a penitentiary. One winter evening my mom and I woke up my sleeping dad when we saw a dark figure in the back yard.

"Get up, get up! There's someone out there," Mom said, as she pulled Dad out of bed. Dad struggled out of bed. Fresh snow had just covered the ground and it was pitch black outside.

"I can't see anything. There's no one there."

"Yes, there is. Someone is standing behind the tree."

We called the police. When they arrived at the house, the stalker ran off. After a little while, one of the officers returned, exhausted. He hadn't caught him. It turned out that the guy had put a ladder up against a tree so he could see into my bedroom window. I wondered if he had been to my house more than once and if he'd come back. The police tried to calm us by saying that stalkers don't usually return to a spot after they have been discovered. This was exactly the case. Luckily, nothing serious ever happened, but sometimes when I was among a lot of fans, I thought about who was there, who was watching me in a certain way. Mikko didn't need to worry about my behavior off the ice since I was always either at school, the ice rink or at home. But rumors could start up out of nothing. One evening Mikko got a call after an event organized by Lumene, one of my sponsors. "Is it true that Kiira has an injury? I heard that Kiira was hurt at an event."

I had performed at the Lumene event on a small synthetic rink and had slipped on some glitter that had been released from the roof. The reporter didn't normally cover skating and so he immediately reported the fall as an injury. But I was amazed that they would make such a big deal about something that happens on the ice dozens of times a day. One thing was for sure: I was at the center of all kinds of attention, wanted and unwanted. Now I was everyone's Kiira. But was I my own Kiira?

7

Paying the Bills

Figure skating is an expensive sport. In Finland many ice rinks are run by their home cities and local clubs hire coaches as full-time employees. The athletes have to pay a yearly membership fee which allows them to attend a set number of training sessions. The outlay is about 6,000 euros a year, and that's not counting travel to competitions and going to international training camps—all of which has to be covered by the skater and their family. That's why in Finland figure skating is a very expensive sport, but compared to the United States, it's cheap. In the States a competitive junior skater's parents can easily spend $500 to $1000 a week! That's because one hour of pro coaching can be anywhere from $100 to $200, at least in big cities.

Before I was able to get sponsors, my family laid out *a lot* of money, and as my career took off, the bills increased exponentially, and Petra was still skating a lot, too. Our "hobby" drained Dad and Mom's wallet; both came from modest middle-class families. Mom was embarrassed to tell her sister how much our skating cost, because for a long time she did not see it as a serious competitive sport and did not quite get how committed I was to achieving my goals.

Dad has always been frugal. He was a hockey coach, but he still was horrified to find out that figure skates with new blades cost well over 500 euros. What? Sometimes Mom would pay for my equipment and fees behind his back. She thought that the financial pressure would ease if and when I got on the national team, but that's not the way it works. When I did get on the national team, we traveled to the Nordic championships in Iceland, a trip which produced a big bill in our mailbox, and there were a number of other fees due after that as well. For a long time my parents continued paying for my trips to international training camps and competitions. These expenses on top of the season membership were a huge drain on the Korpi family finances.

Dad got busy, though. Through his ice hockey connections, Dad knew a lot of corporate people in the Tampere area. He sold ads in the show programs for the Tappara Figure Skaters Christmas and spring performances. Local companies like Tapola were advertised. Tapola sausages were famous across the country, especially their delicious black blood sausage, *mustamakkara*, which was of course on sale at skating and hockey events in my town. That's why it was so special if the audience hung around at halftime of a hockey match to watch me skate as a kid rather than head out and get a *mustakkara*!

At first all the profits from the show program ads went to the club, and Dad was proud to help out, but then came a stroke of good fortune for us. Tappara decided that the middleman could get a percentage of the ad revenue. With this margin, my parents paid many of the bills Petra and I generated. Dad kept working hard to make ends meet, to find me small-scale sponsors and to continue to raise money any way he could. When the Finnish figure skating championships were held at Tampere in 2005, Dad made 750 calls in two weeks and sold more than 1,100 company tickets. Meanwhile, other parents wondered how they could sell even five tickets to their neighbors and relatives.

Our family started seeing signs of financial relief. The owner of the first McDonald's in Finland, Aimo Toimi, liked to go to Tappara hockey games and he enjoyed seeing us skate at halftime. He would give us McDonald's coupons as a friendly gesture. For us skaters those burger coupons were awesome, but my dad made sure we came away with more than just greasy fingers. McDonald's became my first financial supporter in 2005. That's when I appeared in a TV ad for the first time. The partnership with a multinational burger giant was a little troubling for Mom, but it did help with the escalating costs. Every euro was appreciated, and Dad continued to earn a hundred here and a thousand there. His scattershot method of raising money soon became unsustainable, though. When a sponsor contributed more than 5,000 euros, they understandably expected me to be available at their PR events. But that meant that priorities like school and a healthy training schedule would be in jeopardy. That's when a major sponsor stepped in and changed everything.

The person who helped put this together was Hjallis Harkimo. I first met Hjallis at the Torino Olympics in 2006. Hjallis was already a big business and sports influencer in Finland. I didn't know him personally. At one of the Olympic team events he approached me and in his inimitable style said he'd set me up with a Valio thing. Thing? What thing?

7. Paying the Bills

I knew Valio, the major dairy company (called Finlandia Cheese in the States), but I was confused. What was this all about? Dad already knew Hjallis from his ice hockey network. When Dad and I went over to his office, he teased Dad for his endless phone calls and small-time partnerships, which could earn as little as a couple hundred euros. He used Dad's nickname when he gave him advice in a good-natured way.

"Rane, these things are not done by chasing hundreds or even thousands. The situation will become impossible when Kiira needs to satisfy every sponsor."

Even though I was extremely proud of my dad for his huge efforts in keeping us in good financial shape, Hjallis was completely right. Partnership contracts stipulate a number of days that the athlete commits to being available for the company. Typically these organizations demand two to four days a year, depending on the size of the deal. With five partners we are already talking about almost 20 days, which are not easy to fit into the schedule. Hjallis had begun to search for a good, large-scale partner for me after another hockey influencer, Kalervo Kummola, had told him that Dad's deals were not going to do the trick.

Eventually Hjallis landed the Valio sponsorship for me, and I was so appreciative, because now my parents wouldn't have to worry about my skating expenses so much. Valio was not the easiest company for Hjallis to pitch to because they had become very cautious about supporting individual athletes. With hockey star Teemu Selänne and racecar driver Ari Vatanen the company had done well, but sprinter Ben Johnson's doping scandal in 1988 was a hit to their reputation.[*] Valio had largely stepped away from sponsoring top sports for about ten years and had focused its publicity efforts on exercise programs for children and youth throughout Finland. Then, in 2006, following the guidance of a publicity agency and the nudge from Hjallis, Valio began developing a new sponsoring strategy. It featured two main projects: the alpine ski team and me. Alpine skiing and figure skating were technical sports where the risk of doping, which Valio feared most, was small. As for me, at that point, my reputation wasn't quite as spectacular. Sixth place in the European championships and 16th place in the Olympics were not as stellar as the stars of our alpine ski team.

However, Valio figured that my persona fit with their brand perfectly. I apparently represented innocence, authenticity, and, of course,

---

[*] https://www.youtube.com/watch?v=B59oQETne8Y.

Finnishness. Hjallis negotiated a two-year contract with a one-year option. I've been told the deal we made remains one of the biggest ever in individual sports in Finland, apart from Formula 1. Hjallis had pulled off a contract for me that had one zero more than most sponsorships at the time.

No one could have guessed how well everything would go. Not Valio, not Hjallis, and certainly not me. The market research showed that my national recognizability kept rising until it hit almost 100 percent. Once the ads really started coming out, everyone associated me with Valio and probably vice versa. From Valio's point of view they had done really well in building an image for me that seemed to appeal to men and women, young and old alike. The partnership with Valio ended up lasting ten years. By 2008, two years after the Torino Olympics, in addition to Valio, my sponsors included Audi, Finnair, Lumene and Puma. I already had a relationship with Lumene, thanks to Dad (again), and this cosmetics company turned out to be the most long-lasting supporter of my career.

Valio spent quite a bit on me, and I was utilized big time. Maare and Susanna weren't happy about the loss of practice time so they insisted that I do my training sessions in the morning, and only then could I head to Helsinki where the photo shoots and recordings were done. A TV ad for Valio's Vanilla product line was shot at night in the freezing cold practice rink in Hartwall Arena. Directing the shoot was Urban Ström, a Swedish director who had done some of Mary J. Blige's music videos. Petra was my stunt double until I arrived and in the final cut there is a close-up of Petra's skates.

Little by little Mikko took over the work of dealing with my sponsors and the media. Many probably thought that I took on Mikko as my manager only because he was in a relationship with my sister Petra. It wasn't like that—I had started working with Mikko when I first got the Valio contract in 2006. Petra and Mikko met a year later at the world championships in Tokyo. Mikko supported me a lot and we worked together for years. Obviously, the fact that Petra and Mikko lived together helped coordinate everything, and sometimes it felt like my career was a family business.

For a long time, Valio created and maintained my websites. In 2010 my team decided to set up a personal site for me, and we hired the photographer Marko Rantanen for the project. I was really impressed with his images. These were definitely more artsy and fashion-conscious than typical sports photography, which is what we'd been used to seeing on the Valio sites and in the publicity. Rantanen's images are bursting with color, and somehow—I don't know how he does it—every shot is full of movement and energy, even the close-ups. I love his work. Then I thought, "Oh my, maybe these are too glamorous because, man, I don't really *feel* like a star." When the images came out on my website, Valio's marketing manager Hanna Hiekkamies immediately called Mikko to ask if I was thinking of retiring or pulling out of the Valio partnership. Mikko wondered what on earth Hanna was talking about. The people at Valio were worried that I was putting an image out there that was too different from me as that sporty, wholesome Valio girl. Mikko had no intention of breaking off from Valio, but he did want to build a stronger personal brand for me, and yes, that meant to some extent I would not *just* be Valio's Kiira.

We did start to push back a little bit against the classic athlete look. We made agreements with my sponsors that I would not give interviews with tons of logos all over my warm-up jacket. Instead, the logos would be on the wall behind me. Now I, and not my logo-filled warm-up jackets and tops, could represent my sponsors. Most important, our deals

Photographs on my website in 2010 by Marko Rantanen had some people worried I was putting a less than wholesome and sporty image out there.

were financially stable, and Mikko could afford to create a sustainable strategy to keep my team running and give me time to keep practicing in a steady way.

> I was contacted weekly with requests about wanting Kiira to attend different events. Sometimes Kiira was requested to join a company's summer party to host VIP guests, sometimes to the anniversary of a watch shop to give autographs. According to the people requesting, a former Miss Finland would do a similar gig for 500 euros. I politely refused and tried to explain that we have a bit bigger picture with Kiira that we try to manage.—Mikko Luukkaa, manager

The larger companies provided our primary funding, while smaller supporters helped with equipment and my look, such as skate manufacturers, couture firms, and a hairdresser. Mikko helped set all this up, efficiently and with respect on all sides. I'm thankful that my supporters stayed with me for so long even when I didn't always succeed in competitions. According to Mikko, only a handful of Finnish athletes were able to build such a stable and long-lasting network of partners. My yearly revenue went into five figures, something that helped support all the goals we had as a team.

> Apart from Formula 1 drivers, there are maybe five athletes in Finland whose contracts get into real money. Our yearly budget was well into the top five among athletes. Sometimes I would have silly situations where I was offering a partner cooperation with Kiira where for practically half the price, the partner could have got a deal with the whole national team through the federation. However, we never got a large international partner, but we tried. Maybe the problem was that Kiira lacked that Olympic medal.—Mikko Luukkaa, manager

Prize money in my sport isn't exactly something to shout about. That's why sponsor funding is so essential for figure skaters. Competitions with money prizes are rare, and the amounts are modest. The Grand Prix prize awards were the biggest I ever received. The wins earned me $18,000, out of which the Finnish tax service naturally took its share. GP competitions were only held twice a year at most, and additionally a final competition where the six best skaters would go. I was in the GP final as the only Finn (for now) and collected the biggest prize money of my career in the GP series, altogether $33,000 in 2012. That was a substantial addition to my yearly budget, but, of course, it was nothing compared to major cross country and biathlon prizes that are easily more than 100,000 euros. And we're not even talking about those alpine skiers. Ice show work occasionally brought in some extra income—if I managed to fit it into my training and competition schedule. The shows built around the Korean star Yuna Kim were some of the best.

I was invited to Korea for the first time in April 2010. Kim had won Olympic gold that year and I got to experience the hysteria that surrounded her in her home county. The shows were sold out and the arena exits were swamped with fans. There were so many fans that the skaters needed to be escorted out in buses with dark tinted windows and dozens of security guards. I guess that's how rock stars feel. Yuna Kim earned an estimated $10 million per season during her peak years, so it was no wonder that the shows with her name had high compensations for us skaters. I was able to earn quite a bit for one show performance trip to Korea, in contrast to my typical show fees. I was invited to Kim's shows three times in my career, a thrill and an honor.

Over the course of ten years, I received more than $100,000 in athletic grants from the Ministry of Education and Culture in Finland. Annual support ranged from 6,000 to 15,000 euros. In 2009, I was

In Seoul, South Korea, with Mikko and Yuna Kim, 2010.

completely excluded from support money because my total income had gone too high, mostly due to sponsorships, especially the ongoing support from Valio.

I seem to be rattling off numbers with ease here, and you might think I was financially savvy. That's not the way it was. Most of the time I didn't even know how much money I—or, later, my company—had in the bank; Mikko took care of things like that, but I would have wanted him to include me more in the running of my own business. I knew that I needed to build more knowledge and skills around money. I did have some good habits, though. I wasn't a big spender and shopping didn't interest me in the slightest. I have never been particularly fond of material things and couldn't care less if I had an amazing bicycle or bedroom furniture or stylish clothing. When I was younger, my closet was stuffed with training outfits from Puma (a sponsor), a few pairs of jeans and at most a few dresses. If I needed to dress fancy, I would borrow things from Petra. For my first Independence Day at the president's residence, I ordered a dress from the same tailor who sewed my competition outfits. These days, I appreciate craftsmanship and elegant materials and the artistry that goes into making a beautiful wooden desk or the luscious fabrics used in designer clothing.

My attitude toward money came from the way I was raised. At home, we were taught to spend money carefully (and rarely!). Dad is tight with money. He has a tendency to sleep on every purchase and in the morning question whether he really needs that thing or not. He also hoards stuff, especially books and CDs. Back home in Tampere we have two garages full of these treasures. When we were in New York City to celebrate Dad's 60th, Petra and I were annoyed by my parents' constant commentary about restaurant prices. I can understand where they're coming from. My parents did have some tough years, but sometimes it's OK not to count every penny.

There were a lot of conflicting emotions, shame and pride, guilt and relief, around money. My attitude about money was like other areas of my life in which I was deeply conflicted: publicity, my wins and losses, body image, and lots more. Basically, I couldn't fully appreciate what I was earning because my attitude toward money was unhealthy. That created even more pressure to outperform at competitions. I felt I needed to prove that I deserved my financial success. I felt responsible to so many people. I knew that if my earnings were good, then my team and I would benefit. In Finnish culture you're not supposed to show off any financial success, and my sponsors had an interest in keeping my public profile likable and modest. Being young and unsure of my center, I actually looked to the public Kiira as a guide for how to be! This probably happens with a lot of young people who are suddenly in the public eye. In my case, there was another problem. Once I achieved a level of financial success everyone wanted a piece of me. In other words, I was not ready to establish myself as an independent person with ownership of my own career, money, and achievements.

It has taken me a long time to acknowledge my limiting, deep-seated beliefs about money. For years I did not see my work or time as fully mine. Unfortunately, I valued my efforts according to how valuable others perceived them to be. Gradually I'm freeing myself from the sadness, guilt, and lack of clarity regarding my feelings about money. I'm gaining confidence in my ability to create work on my own terms and the financial abundance that comes with it. I still want my success to have a positive impact on the people around me and in the world, but in a way that is consonant with who I am and what my priorities are.

8

Those Triple Jumps Hiding in Warsaw

For a long time, the idea of being tired was foreign to me. Before the Torino Olympics in February 2006, I was up for anything, especially to get out there and perform. But by December, something inside was changing, and it wasn't good. Maybe I packed in too many events that year. The first symptoms of fatigue appeared right after the Olympics, which would be understandable, but I never got the chance to recover properly. The minute we got back home we had to start getting ready for the world championships. They were coming up in March and we'd be flying out to Calgary, in Alberta, Canada. It wasn't easy to hunker down to work again. After all, I went from the thrill of the Olympics back to my local practice rink in Hervanta, a suburb of Tampere. I recognized the feelings of exhaustion rising up but got right down to work. Were the early results showing that my toughness was paying off, or was I running on fumes? In Calgary I did a triple-triple combination for the first time in a competition, and I placed 10th at the 2006 world championships.

Then, I got a surprise invitation to Japan. It was an invitation-only competition for three teams, and I was invited to join the European team with Sarah Meier and Stéphane Lambiel from Switzerland and Alexei Yagudin from Russia. Lambiel had just won WC gold in Calgary and Yagudin was cooling off his career after Olympic gold and three world championship wins. Sarah and I were still without medals at international championships. The timing of the competition was not great— by late spring it's time to recover—but no way was I going to turn down the opportunity to be on such a great team. It was an honor to travel with them, not to mention the prize money. We ended up placing second, which meant a $15,000 check for each of us. However, ramping up for this event meant that my winter season, which should have come to a close in March, stretched all the way into May.

In the fall, it became harder and harder to focus. I won the Finlandia Trophy in October, but with relatively weak programs. Still, it was the first time that I placed higher than my idol Susanna Pöykiö in any competition. Then, I jammed *six more* competitions into my schedule before Christmas. I missed tons of schoolwork and exams. I was in my second year of high school and wanted to do well, so I devoted every shred of free time to catching up. Also, I needed to do events for my sponsors, and so I never got any down time. Then there was a Grand Prix competition in Moscow. I went and skated, but my concentration was shot. When the Finnish championships came up in December, the situation became straight-up scary.

I remember seeing myself on the screen in the middle of the program. I drifted on the ice in a half-dream and was distracted by my own image. Oh yeah, the Lutz is coming now, OK. Whoopsie. I popped the Lutz—instead of a triple jump I managed only one rotation. And what is my next jump again? The more I tried to focus, the less I could feel the ice. I had never experienced anything like this before.

That season was rough. At times, I was so tired that I might sleep 10 to 11 hours at night, which wasn't at all normal for me. My time management was out of control and my training discipline was completely disrupted. And at the Finnish championships I finished fourth, a disaster.

> I was the one setting the ground rules and demanded that in addition to training, Kiira had to keep up with her usual schoolwork and, of course, chores at home, too. I didn't act as if we had a figure skater growing up at home but a young high school student who would have an academic career. Somehow, in the midst of all the activity and excitement, I didn't see Kiira's exhaustion.—Brita Korpi, mother

By Christmastime, we were planning for the 2007 European championships, which were coming up fast, in late January 2007 in Warsaw, Poland. I was shattered emotionally and physically. I didn't know what to do. Luckily, I had already qualified for my spot on the Finnish women's team, but the situation didn't look good. I had not skated one clean competition all fall. The flu and the sinusitis that lingered into January was not fun, either. Maare and Susanna were worried. But I had frequently gone into competitions ill or not fully prepared. Would I be able to pull off a miracle again?

The come-from-behind approach was almost routine already. In fact, I was under the crazy impression that the opposite could be true, that if I was too well prepared, I'd do worse. At least this is what I had convinced myself of. For a while there really *were* miracles on the ice. When things were rough and my team started worrying, I would dig deep for the strength I needed. This is exactly what I hoped would happen in Warsaw. Somehow jumps that I'd never been able to do consistently, even in training, would just happen, as if they had been hiding somewhere inside me. Right?

When we got to Warsaw, I had Lutz and flip jumps planned for the beginning of my program. Of the six figure-skating jumps these two jumps generate the most points, but we weren't sure if I could execute these well. I knew exactly how to do those jumps but at that point I was having problems executing them well, even in practice. So we switched to the loop as the opener for both my programs. Still, I dreamed of upping my game, and there were guardian angels on my side, after all. Their names were Tarja and Maare.

Tarja Ristanen had been chosen captain of the Finnish team for the second time in a row, and she had arrived in Warsaw before us. When Maare got to her hotel room from the airport, she saw a text message.

"I am here at Warsaw's skating arena and you will never guess what I saw under a staircase. Kiira's triple flip."

Tarja was another fine skater who had been Maare's student at one time, like basically every other skater in Finland! The next day Maare got another message from Tarja.

"I went to the restaurant. There, eating at the next table, was Kiira's triple Lutz."

Maare laughed at the messages and showed them to me.

"Kiira, look at these sweet messages from Tarja. The jumps are *there*, waiting for you. Off we go."

In the next competition practice I did my programs as planned, with the easier jumps to kick off: My axel, Salchow, toe loop and loop. In between I blew snot out of my runny nose as I skated up to Maare to get some advice.

Maare said simply, ""All right, fine. Now your flip." I built up speed and jumped a successful triple flip. Oh my God.

"Now your triple Lutz."

Just like that, I did a clean triple Lutz. I had not made these two jumps cleanly for almost the whole season, but there I was, a day before the European championships, and they just happened. I could see Maare there at the edge of the rink, weeping.

Tarja walked up behind her and whispered, "Ease up on the tears. The other coaches and the judges are wondering what's going on here."

Maare prayed that the same touch that found me in practice would stay with me through the competition. On the day of the competition, she was there, ready. Right before I launched in front of the cameras and the crowd, she said in my ear, "Do those jumps, sweetie, just do them." And I did. In my short program, I completed a triple flip and the others, too—it was the best short program of my season.

I placed a very surprising fifth after the short program, leaving fellow Finns Sussu and Alisa behind. Once again, I managed to perform at my best in a competition even though (or because!) I had come in with doubts and in not the best physical shape. After the short program, I was only one point away from bronze. Why, I don't know, but when the day came, I skated my free program with wildness and courage. When it was over, I thought it had been a beautiful mess. I couldn't imagine getting a medal after that. Neither did my team.

A miracle. My first major competition medal. A bronze right behind Carolina Kostner and Sarah Meier. I became the second Finn in female figure skating ever to medal in international championships. Only Sussu had done this before. At this event she finished fourth and Alisa sixth. Finland was by far the best country overall, and even Alisa placed higher than the best Russian skater of the competition. Russian figure skating was in deep water at that time.

> I believe that Kiira's optimism and ability to think positively took her really far. She could perform beyond herself even when she came into a competition seriously struggling. If you don't believe that anything is possible, it then isn't possible. Maare and Kiira were optimistic, too much, I thought. It was me who often brought them back down to earth. But now I'm tipping my hat to optimism.—Susanna Haarala, Kiira's coach, 2002–2013

It was unbelievable that this all happened after such a crazy season. I had been happy just to be part of the team. Mom was celebrating in the audience; it was the first international championships that she saw live. She was usually too nervous to watch my competitions live and didn't usually tour with me. Even in Finland at our club's local competitions, Mom would rather sell chocolate brownies in the arena corridors than sit in the audience.

My career could not be described with the word "consistency."

My first European medal, bronze in Warsaw, 2007 (Elina Paasonen / Aamulehti).

I needed to go to the bottom so I could rise up again. But there was another, darker dimension to success. In my mind, it wasn't really mine. In my mind, I needed to pay a debt, and keep paying. The EC medal gave me a momentary feeling that I had finally fulfilled everyone's wishes, fulfilled all those expectations, but this was shortlived. Soon my contentment faded with the onrush of new goals, new plans. I needed to start getting ready for the world championships and for my final exams. After all, I was trying to finish high school.

But there was still magic at the core. Things were complicated, but I knew that somewhere in my heart was something pure, something special, and always that deep joy around the ice. Skating provided an opportunity for me to feel a deep sense of connectedness and belonging to something greater than the material world. It was so hard to get to that core, though, and hard to know what it was that worked to keep me strong, what it was that broke me down. I sometimes think about what my career would have been like if I had not achieved success so early—If I had toured junior competitions a bit longer and had a few more years to mature before the publicity crashed on us and the expectations piled on. But at the same time, the wins built my confidence. I do feel that the early experiences of success and the success on the European championship ice in 2007 carried me through the most difficult times to come. Without those experiences, my belief in success might have died out sooner.

⇉ 9 ⇇

Weight Watcher

My relationship with food and body image went in unhealthy directions after the EC bronze in spring 2007. Until then I had eaten almost anything without paying too much attention, or at least that's how I remember it. One thing is for sure, as a kid I ate with gusto, and it helps that home-cooked Finnish food is awesome. My favorite food as a child was Granny's meat sauce, so tasty I would slurp every last drop from the plate. As a little girl, I gobbled up all the fatty bits of our Christmas baked ham till the grease ran down my cheeks.

I'm not a great cook. Even boiling a potato was challenging for me. I was in the sixth grade when Mom needed to take a work call one evening. The potatoes were boiling on the stove, but where was Kiira? When Mom stepped back into the kitchen, she found the pot smoking and some burnt black things at the bottom. Mom was boiling with anger. Why hadn't I known to add more water?

"You know I can't cook potatoes," I said in my typical challenging voice.

"All right. Then there will be no training tomorrow and Kiira Korpi will come home and learn to make potatoes."

I thought Mom was bluffing but the next day she came to pick me up in the middle of ice practice. We had a competition coming up, but she didn't care. Luckily, she got stuck talking to another skating parent and the ice practice finished before she marched me home for a potato-boiling lesson.

We weren't a family that would gather together for dinner every day. A lot of times, Petra and I heated up our own meals when we came home from practice. Aside from the occasional Jacky pudding, sweets were rare. At skating camp I would feast on candy to make up for it. Laura always had bags of the stuff. Then there was that five-kilo summer back in 2004. Laura and I were at Lake Arrowhead, California. We

70

were staying in a small trailer near the training center. The cooking facilities were as limited as our skills. It was a summer of candy and instant this and instant that. Lots of chicken nuggets and French fries. No wonder I returned to Finland that fall packing an extra 10 pounds. Back then, my relationship with food and even with skating was more carefree so it didn't bother me that much. The weight quickly disappeared once I returned to my home diet and steady training. Our chicken nugget summer was fun while it lasted.

When I started consciously dieting in spring 2007, things changed, and not in a good way. I became obsessed with how I could improve as an athlete and that was my justification for fooling around with my food choices. I picked up a description of a "professional" nutrition plan. I remember Susanna Pöykiö telling me about her super-detailed diet plan at the world championships in Japan in 2007. Her words stuck with me because this was Sussu talking. I was getting all kinds of messages and expectations that messed with my body image. It also didn't help that I unconsciously modeled my mom's not-so-positive relationship with her body image and eating habits. I had launched into the public eye at the age of 16 and was exposed to both flattery and insults, and that influenced me, too. To outsiders it looked like I was eating normally, but in my head, I was counting calories with every bite. At the scale I worried over every slight change in the numbers. I weighed myself every day, sometimes many times a day for eight years. After my competitive career was over, one of my challenges was to try and break this habit.

I was good at losing weight, and in 2007 I slimmed down dramatically. At the 2008 world championships in Göteborg, I was outright scrawny. I'm still shocked when I look at those photos. I went on a holiday in Malaysia right after the competition to see Petra, who was studying there. From the bikini pictures it's clear I had pared away every last gram of fat. I was only 50 kilos (I'm almost 5'7"). Two seasons before I had weighed 58! That's a difference of about 20 pounds! Later my competition weight settled in the range of 52–54 kilos.

I wasn't the only one obsessing about weight. When I saw Laura at the Göteburg world championships she didn't come with her bags of candy. No candy?! That was a sign of how serious we both had become about our chosen sport. It's definitely important to think about weight as a figure skater, but when does it become unhealthy? We never said a word about it. We knew the name of the game. Mealtimes were not the same as they used to be. I would eye how much tomato sauce Laura put on her pasta and how much dressing on her salad and I'll bet she eyed me, too. Laura and I were a lot alike, and we influenced each other in both good and bad ways.

My slimmer profile in the mirror gave me pleasure at first; I can't deny that. At practice, my jumps felt lighter. At the same time there was a mismatch between what I perceived and what was real. I was very thin but did not see myself that way. Instead, I always found some flaw to fix. As time went on, I began developing stomach issues. Sometimes I couldn't eat at all. Sometimes I looked as if I was pregnant because my belly was bloated. Sometimes food would just run through me, and I would go to the toilet ten times a day. I went to the doctor and was diagnosed with esophagitis, and I thought OK, that's all it is. No problem, right? Wrong. As I continued to deprive myself of nutrients, my body withered and shrank.

My willpower was strong but so was my self-criticism. I forbade myself desserts or sweets, and if I had a small piece of cake at a party, I would feel terribly guilty afterward. The fear of gaining weight was overwhelming. I had nightmares where the scariest thing was eating a forbidden cookie or getting a brutal glance from my coach because I had gained a gram or two. The nightmares would come back even after I stopped competing.

In the spring and summer of 2008 things got worse, and the collapse came in the fall, when the annual test camp for the national team was held in Vierumäki. The program included, among other things, a vertical jump test on a special mat, pull-ups, and rabbit running, where you're supposed to run after an accelerating light for as long as you can.

They also measured our weight and BFP (body fat percentage). I had taken fitness tests for many years, so I knew what they were all about. Usually I did well. This time, my body failed me. After the tests my legs were cramping up and pretty much shut down. Days and weeks went by, and I was still completely burned out. I'd tearfully call Mom from the grocery store so she could drive me home because walking a mile back to our house was impossible.

The scariest thing was that no one knew what was going on with me. I couldn't skate for almost a month. My season start got pushed back as I cancelled competitions one after the other. I went to see every possible doctor and specialist, but they were missing some key information. I never told any of them about my one-woman diet plan because I thought, well, that's just how an athlete should eat. For a long time, my

72

temperature was elevated, which means that the overall strain had been way too much. I got tested for overtraining but nothing exceptional was found there either. Rheumatism tests and neural pathway tests were normal. Celiac disease was ruled out. I underwent a colonoscopy. We tried acupuncture, reflexology, and massage, but nothing helped. In the media there was talk of burnout and anorexia. We were all worried. Nothing like this had ever happened to me. Finally, one doctor delivered a vague diagnosis: overload of the somatic nervous system. What did that mean? Not very helpful.

> We walked around the block arm in arm, and I knew something was horribly wrong then. I had always been for her finishing school, going to see grandparents, doing housework but I saw that it was all too much at that moment. Everyone wanted something from Kiira. Mom wants, coach wants, school wants ... it was too much.—Brita Korpi, mother

Now when I think back, I can clearly see that my body simply couldn't handle any more. Too much training, too little nutrition and too little rest. At the same time there were my final exams at high school and the added stress of entrance exams for university.

I think that my eating patterns in those early days were a major cause of the many injuries later in my career. Years later I went to see a nutritional advisor. It's unbelievable that I waited until 2012 to speak with Patrik Borg, a person I should have sought out earlier and should have listened to more seriously. He informed me that everyone has an ideal weight range at which the body operates at its peak. It is important to not try to maintain a weight at the lower end of the range for extended periods. This wasn't rocket science; I understood this basic principle as a young athlete, and probably a lot of people tried to give me solid advice, but I wasn't hearing them. I went on stubbornly with my habitual undereating.

The problem wasn't all in my head. Hanging around other skaters and very critical coaches, I was very aware of the comments and the staring. I'm sure this is very common in sports like figure skating and gymnastics. It's not that the young athletes don't rationally know the importance of eating enough, but we're part of a culture of unhealthy body image. In response to all the pressure, young skaters will do everything they can to conform to the idea of the "perfect" body type. Instead of making decisions based on science and professional advice, I was way too influenced by the opinion of peers, pundits, coaches, bloggers, and the media. So the crazy calorie counting at meals continued, with every single bite. Even today, I might look at a piece of food and a number pops up.

There was a whole range of bad effects on my body, including my hormones. My periods started coming inconsistently, and so I used birth control pills to even things out, but I didn't know this only covers up the real problems that come when you starve yourself, such as lower bone density and a drop in your estrogen levels. OK, I achieved temporarily a feeling of lightness when I jumped, but at what cost? The tragic thing is that I never again scored as well in my fitness tests, never hitting the levels I had, for instance, during the Torino 2006 Olympic season. I was paying a heavy price to get a certain number on the scale and the so-called ideal "look" on the ice.

> The self-consciousness of girls is on another level than, for example, boys that play hockey. When boys start to get tired, they often throw in the towel. With girls this is not the case, and the strain and fatigue build up to dangerous levels. Then recovery and restoring strength takes a really long time— if at all. There are cases where it never does. These factors were present also in Kiira's case; her devotion was strong. School and training filled her days. I believe that the balance between training and recovery was skewed, and in the long run the regulatory systems of the body started to become overwhelmed.—Rauno Korpi, father

The recovery problems with my legs only started to ease as the 2008 Finnish championships got closer. I got crucial help from physiotherapist Jarmo "Jami" Ahonen, who was recommended by Susanna Rahkamo. Susanna was the president of the Finnish Figure Skating Association and a former ice dance world championship medalist with her partner Petri Kokko. Jami is a top professional in his field and was the Finnish Olympic team's physiotherapist at seven Olympics. He also worked for almost 30 years with the dancers of the Finnish National Ballet. He has also worked with some of our top athletes, including tennis player Jarkko Nieminen.

I was surprised by how Jami worked on me. He didn't touch my cramping legs at all, but instead concentrated on my stomach area. It was rock hard. Jami worked the hip flexors that attach to the lower abdomen. They were tight and blocked, and then I started to feel the blood flowing into my legs. It was a great feeling! I had been running from one specialist to another, and no one had realized that my leg condition was symptomatic of what was going on in my belly area. So many of my physical problems seemed to be related to this part of my body. From this moment onward I began a partnership with Jami that lasted to the very end of my career. I had found someone who was the ultimate professional in his field and whom I could trust. Meeting Jami was the best thing to come out of that phase of unhealthy eating and dieting.

Before the European championships in Bern in December 2010 I was struggling with some triple jumps. I wasn't leaping neatly enough. Susanna, Maare and I wracked our brains trying to figure out why. I had started going to a nutritionist again. I thought that I had been eating really well. I ate a lot of nuts and had plenty of fruit smoothies. With the more sensible nutrition the stomach issues had gradually been clearing up, so what was going on?

"Have you been checking your weight?" Susanna asked when we couldn't find a clear reason for the jumping problems.

Are you kidding? Of course I had. The scale showed a few kilos more than my normal competition weight. I thought it was due to bloating and normal hormonal changes, and I clung to the idea that it was a temporary thing. Then, when I thought about the previous couple of months, I realized I had gained baseline weight—two kilos! Oh my God! I was so mad at Susanna and Maare that they hadn't said anything about it before. Two kilos!

Susanna tried to calm me: "That's not a number that's noticeable, but it might change the way you feel."

I had failed as an athlete and as a person. How could I have let myself put on two kilos? How did the coaches and I miss this? I was sure that everyone could notice that I was fat (I thought). I started to diet again, and Susanna seemed happy about that. I kept up a strict food intake regimen until the European championships in January, and by then I'd managed to squeeze off the two extra kilos. A diet is not at all the best way to prepare for a competition, but it maybe did contribute to getting me that European bronze. Who knows, maybe I would have had more stamina in my free program if I hadn't lost all that weight. When I won the two Grand Prix gold medals, in Paris in 2010 and Moscow in 2012, I was heavier than my average competition weight, but I still skated both the short and long programs really well!

Anyway, going back to what Patrik said, it's not a problem if you want to be a bit lighter for a short period of time during the most crucial competitions. The problems come back big time when you don't return to a healthier weight afterward. That's when the hormone levels are telling you something is really wrong. Like I said, skaters get incomplete information and sometimes really bad advice from coaches, judges, officials, and fellow athletes. To try to be super skinny 365 days a year is crazy. Our overall training should be guided by real science and a sense of balance. I know that, for example, in Australia there are some guidelines for female long-distance runners. They're not allowed to move on to the next training phase after a competition season unless their periods have returned to normal. Maybe there is something to be learned from that in the skating world?

Another place where we need change is in coaching. When it comes to nutrition, coaches are dealing with young skaters who are even more self-conscious about body image and diet than many people of that age, and some coaches do not manage it well. I mean, on the one hand, body weight does play a role in figure skating. It is easier to send a lighter object into the air than a heavier object. But jumping power is about so much more than how many kilos you weigh! It would be wiser to look at the muscle-fat ratio than be just fixated on the number on the scale. Most of all, I think we should pay much more attention to how strong, light and energetic the skater *feels* rather than how they look.

It's no surprise that looks play a big role in figure skating. This brings us to issues of diversity and inclusion. Historically, skaters of color have basically had to skate twice as well as anyone else if they have wanted to even dream about getting high scores from the judges. Mistreatment may happen also if you look "too big" (meaning, not looking starved) or "too different" in one way or the other. At the ice arena, the most common comments are often about your appearance. If a skater is thin the assumption is that they have trained well. Conversely, if someone looks a bit heavier, people might assume they are lax or lazy. That's what skaters have to put up with, where both positive and negative comments work against us because they distract the skater from the reality of their fitness level and true state of preparation. Sometimes we're there, but because of the spotlight and nonstop chatter, we don't think we are. This is why it's so important to be centered in who you are.

I received praise for my thin looks from sports journalists, coaches, and many more people, sometimes ironically when I'd been ill for a long period. This shows how superficial these comments can be and that it's important that young athletes not be exposed to this language, especially by people they trust. For example, at a training camp one summer, Alexei Mishin said I was *now* "looking really good," after I had been suffering from serious stomach issues*: "Good, good, Kiira. Now you are looking really good."

Yeah, right. If only he'd known that I had not eaten for days. Actually, I suspect he did know that because I'd been away from the ice for a few days and even had to visit the hospital to get on intravenous drip.

Some coaches were quite blunt about weight goals and others more diplomatic, but the key point is that the young athlete is so self-conscious and typically wants to do anything to please the coach, whom they trust blindly. Even a hint of a comment by someone would send me into a spiral of harsh self-discipline. Sometimes all it took was a look, a disgusted, disapproving gaze directed at me or an indirect question like "Have you been enjoying life too much lately?" Back to the diet!

In California coach Rafael Arutyunyan was strict about the weight of all his skaters. He had a habit of hugging skaters while checking the thickness of the "fat layer" on the rib cage. I wish I had been more assertive back then. This kind of behavior violated my physical space and integrity. The coach should not be allowed to touch a skater like that without asking permission, let alone measure so-called "fat layers." Rafael also didn't hesitate to make some direct comments. In 2013 at the national team camp in Vierumäki, Rafael said, "Kiira, you need to be in better shape!"

I had been injured and was probably a few kilos heavier than my usual competition weight. This is all it took to throw me back into my obsessive dieting!

What irks me is why wouldn't some of the best coaches in the world want to work with the best nutrition experts? And when will they stop giving amateur advice on eating? One of Rafael's former skaters, Adam Rippon, said in an interview that Rafael pressured him to lose weight. He only realized how unsustainable this lifestyle of trying to get by with three pieces of bread per day was when he got a stress fracture.[†] Adam has said he thinks the injury was clearly due to lack of nutrients in his body. After he started working with a professional nutritionist, he gained ten pounds (muscle!) and was able to perform at a much higher level! I wish coaches and judges and skating organizations would take responsibility and not encourage dangerous eating habits or unhealthy weight loss techniques. And I hope that the skaters starting from a very

---

* A legendary Russian coach who worked with Evgeni Plushenko and countless other champions. https://en.wikipedia.org/wiki/Alexei_Mishin.

† https://www.nytimes.com/2018/02/13/sports/olympics/figure-skating-adam-rippon.html.

young age would be taught to take ownership of their own bodies and minds. They should be encouraged and taught how not to allow destructive and mixed messages to shake their inner power and self-worth.

One more muffin, maybe just one more. Oops, I ate ten! My relationship with food was way out of balance, alarmingly out of balance, and in between periods of super-strict dieting, I'd binge. I might go for cinnamon buns, candy, white bread, butter, cheese—I'd clear out the fridge or the freezer. There were times I ate so much that I couldn't fit one more thing. I remember my tummy aching unbearably, and I would run to the bathroom to stick my fingers down my throat. I never managed to actually puke; I just suffered with a bloated, aching stomach all day. I'm glad I wasn't able to throw up then because that would've launched me on the path to bulimia. That's not to say I wasn't already showing signs of a serious disorder.

I never talked about this because I was so ashamed of my lack of discipline. I didn't realize that my body was screaming for more food!

> Although I sometimes saw that Kiira was having a hard time, we never really talked about it. I was under the impression that as the sister of the star athlete my role was to urge her on, encourage her. Perhaps I should have asked more often, simply, "How are you? Is everything OK?"—Petra Korpi, older sister

Because my weight never got under a certain number, I thought I couldn't possibly be eating too little. One time Susanna saw me eating the *whole* tiny meal during a flight and said I should be grateful for being able to eat *that* much so there was yet another reason why I couldn't see what was truly going on with me—if Susanna thinks I eat too much, then yeah, it's OK to diet. Of course, if I had taken a sane minute to compare the calorie intake versus energy consumption, it would've been clear that I wasn't eating enough, but that wasn't as important as the number on the scale, right? Human beings are great at coming up with excuses, especially when they're dealing with an addiction or illness. My weight isn't going down, so I must be eating normally. Yesterday I ate a chocolate bar. I'm not that scrawny. Right.

Unfortunately, orthorexia and bulimia are very common in figure skating, and there are many cases of anorexia too. The winner of the team competition in the Sochi Winter Olympics, Yulia Lipnitskaya, was one of the first Russian Team Tutberidze skaters to speak openly about her anorexia. The United States' Gracie Gold's future was supposed to be golden, but in the fall of 2017, she said that she was suffering from depression, anxiety, and an eating disorder.* These are just two examples. Adam Rippon and others show that the problem is not limited to one gender.

Recently I've learned how common it is for many skaters to not only use throwing up as a strategy for maintaining weight but also use laxatives and water pills to remove the "extra" from the body during a competition. According to an interview, the 2018 Olympic champion, the then-16-year-old Alina Zagitova didn't drink water at all during the Olympics, she just rinsed her mouth.† In another interview she said her answer to managing weight change in puberty was to just close her mouth and not eat, or to eat, but just a little bit. I've heard that the weight control in some skating schools goes to extreme levels (they may weigh you every single day, and if the number is a hundred grams more than yesterday, you might be forbidden to eat or forced to train more), and for sure, these kinds of public statements only confirm that we have an *extremely* serious problem here.

Although I was never formally diagnosed with an eating disorder, I think it's important to realize that systemic issues in any sport can take many forms and can do a lot of damage to the health and well-being of up-and-coming athletes. In figure skating there is an obvious value to slimming down in order to execute many of the more difficult jumps. Skating coaches, judges and other people will encourage weight management—all understandable *if* (!) it's done wisely with professionals who actually know about nutrition and long-term health effects of certain weight management strategies. The RED-S syndrome (relative energy deficiency in sports) is a very real problem among athletes of all genders across many different sports. It can lead to early osteoporosis, heart problems, frequent injuries and illness, irregular or missing periods for female athletes and reduced testosterone for male athletes, among other consequences such as mood disorders, reduced motivation and focus, and poorer performance over the long run. I'm hoping all these things will be discussed very seriously among all the stakeholders

---

* American skater Gracie Gold came out with a story about her eating disorder in 2019. https://www.facebook.com/watch/?v=483631842269696.

† https://deadspin.com/alina-zagitova-says-she-didnt-drink-water-during-the-20-1832459869.

in my beloved sport, because we want our athletes to be thriving and to be able to have a healthy life *before, during,* and *after* their competitive careers. Unfortunately, I know many former athletes who haven't been able to continue doing sports or have children because of the ordeals they put their bodies through.

Nowadays, I try to eat healthy. I can still turn on my self-discipline machine but repurposed toward a more balanced lifestyle. My organs, blood vessels, and muscles have mostly recovered from my earlier days, but my joints and bones seem to have taken a bigger hit. I can't run or jog for very long without experiencing hip, knee and ankle pain. I'm happy that my hormonal health has also returned to normal. I'm also grateful that I'm still able to skate (without the big jumps), play tennis and be active in many ways without being in pain.

Changing my eating habits after my competitive career has been tough. It's not easy to rewire your mind! At times, I still have the urge to patrol my eating or my weight, particularly when I'm going through a stressful life situation or if I get a comment about my weight from someone I care about. Sometimes I'm fooled by passing thoughts, say, when I'm shopping for clothes that I'm the biggest, laziest loser because I've gained weight since my competition days. But then my reasonable brain kicks in and I can tune into how much stronger, healthier and more alive I now *feel*. I knowingly practice a compassionate relationship with myself and try to listen to my body's needs, although I admit it's hard! I've made a deal with myself that I would give myself at least the chance to eat sufficiently and live in a bigger body, and if after a year or so I don't *feel* more powerful, healthy, strong, feminine, fierce, light and grounded, I can always retreat to my restrictive way of being and living in a smaller body.

≈ 10 ≈

282 Jumps

We practiced thousands of hours with Kiira at the Hervanta ice rink. In figure skating, the training is very solitary. Finnish figure skaters practice so much alone. Sparring would be really important.—Susanna Haarala, Kiira's coach, 2002–2013

In the early 2000s, figure skating in Finland was not yet hugely popular. Great skaters such as Susanna Rahkamo and Petri Kokko were well-known, but the fine points of scoring and technique were still a mystery to our audiences, not to mention to sports journalists. I would try to explain how tough our training was. I practiced six days a week, usually with Sunday off. There were typically 10 ice practice sessions a week and off-ice routines on top of that. I was obsessed with documenting everything. In the 2010–2011 season, I did 394 hours of on-ice training, 315 hours off-ice, not counting warm-ups and cool downs, and 117 hours recovery training. There were also lots of stretching routines and therapeutic massages. Then, with schoolwork, I was left with almost no time at all. At school, the rumor was that Kiira couldn't even find her way to Hämeenkatu, our "Main Street," where teens would gather in the evenings.

The training calendar for figure skaters starts in late March, right after the world championships, after a one-week break. This is the "preparatory phase," and it lasts about six to eight weeks. The programs for the next skating season are designed. In terms of physical work, we work on strength and endurance. In the first 30 seconds of the four-minute free program, the heart rate rises close to maximum and stays there for practically the whole time, so in addition to explosiveness, the sport also takes great endurance. This was a challenge for me as I am constitutionally a fast-twitch athlete. I have never been in love with running but I did get my endurance up to a decent level. In the prep phase we also worked on skating fundamentals. That meant some honest troubleshooting. We tuned up things like posture and skating speed.

81

Because we were doing intensive strength and endurance work, no new techniques or jumps were learned during prep.

Then, from early June through July, we shifted into the first part of summer training season. That's when we learned new jumps and our gym regimen took a backseat to the ice work. In my case, I needed to add mobility exercises because flexibility was never my forte, but other than that, practice outside the rink became light. In figure skating, it's not a good idea to do much heavy strength training during the competition season or the pre-competition phase, because having tight and sore muscles for days would interfere with the demanding work on the ice. However, I was lucky to have far-sighted Susanna by my side. She created a balanced and tough set of exercises timed perfectly over the course of a year and so I believed I was getting the best overall conditioning. Susanna created brutally difficult and brutally effective hurdle exercises for jumps. My agility and motor skills grew as well as my core strength and control. One season Susanna tried moving all jumping exercises to the ice, but quickly noticed that in tests, my off-ice jumps grew weaker. That was because skating jumps on the ice are rarely executed at full strength because they are more about rotation and technical skills, and so my muscles were not being challenged in a way that kept up maximum strength. We went back to a steady routine of strength training off-ice.

Susanna's approach was having a positive effect and could be measured with the special tests I took at Viermäki every year. That first year with Susanna, results were great. I was excited about my stats on the most important metric in our sport, the one-leg speed jump. At my best I jumped 53.7 centimeters. That's a lot for a skater! My pull-up and ab crunch numbers weren't too bad either. Susanna had helped me build some good muscle tone, but this was all before my unhealthy decisions around dieting started to gradually weaken my body.

The second summer training phase was typically at a special camp abroad, without my coaches. Finnish coaches usually take leave in the summer. So even at the age of 14, 15, I was off to camps in California or Switzerland on my own. Susanna and Maare crossed their fingers that I would remember to keep some sort of training diary so that they would know where to pick up in the fall. I wonder sometimes about the wisdom of sending kids abroad at this age without their primary coaches. It's not just about being a minor but about the sorts of ideas I got in my head. It's one thing to be inspired by skaters from around the world, but it's another to make unhealthy comparisons and build unrealistic expectations. At the international camps I noticed that other figure skaters didn't take as much time off as I had been. The American figure skaters I knew didn't seem to have a proper holiday break, even in the summer. They practiced all year long, and I witnessed a lot of other athletes really extending themselves, too—maybe overextending themselves. Was this good?

In any case, when I got back home my rhythms were thrown off. In my early teens, before my encounters with young athletes at the camps, my Christmas break used to be pleasant, and I squeezed in a fun week here and there in the spring. But then, as time went on, I started feeling guilty and anxious at all the wrong times. I became restless during the holidays. After only two days with no training I started to feel physically uneasy and mentally unsettled. Things were upside down. I yearned to train during my breaks and yearned to take breaks during training. I wasn't alone in my feelings and knew a lot of ambitious young people like me were driven, too, and they were making some big sacrifices for their goals. It was much harder to rest smart than to train smart.

After the summer camp training and a very brief break before competition season, training picked up again in the fall with "pre-competition" trainings. At this point we worked on new element repetitions, and the aim was to incorporate some of the new technical things I had learned during the summer. Physically the aim then was to improve endurance—in other words, to stay strong up to the very last seconds of a program.

> Working with Kiira opened my eyes to trends I had been observing and thinking about for a while. I have spent hundreds of hours in ice arenas and noted in my journal everything that the top skaters of the world were doing and how they practiced. I then chose things to implement in Kiira's training. Throughout my career, I have learned immensely, and I am really thankful for that.—Maaret Siromaa, Kiira's coach, 1996–2013

I wasn't the only one who was wowed and a little intimidated by the quality and commitment of skaters on the international scene. Susanna and Maare had also seen how elite skaters from Japan, Russia, and the United States did all the technically difficult and physically demanding elements in the competition practices, sometimes even a couple of hours before the competition. We assumed that their at-home practices were even harder. Now my whole team was committed to ramping up my training. We knew it needed to be done gradually, to protect my body, but we also knew I needed to up my game. During the 2009–2010 season, I skated my short program through 57 times and free program 36 times. In the spring of 2010, ramping up for the Olympics, I did 282 jumps in a week and that's without counting warm-up jumps.

Our long-range plan was not only to increase the hours on the ice and to add more full run-throughs of my programs. Because of the physical strain, I could only do a full run-through once in an hour-long ice practice session, so we did individual elements over and over. This plan was put into effect in the 2010–2011 season. I went fully through 99 short programs and 79 free programs. That's 178 times, the equivalent of skating for 10 hours at maximum heart rate while having to keep a big smile—the all-important smile! The increased workload showed up in my results, and in 2011, I medaled in the European championships after a four-year break.

I diligently kept track of everything, not just in my diary but on an Excel spreadsheet where I calculated categories and quantities of jumps and success rates. The triple Lutz continued to be a huge challenge with typically only 20 percent of my landings sticking. After slamming to the ice so many times, I also recorded some less than pretty things in my diary—sore sternums, stiff vertebra, and bruised tailbones. But I kept on smiling.

⇒ 11 ⇐

Imperfect Perfectionist

- Emotional, with a lot of strength.
- Ambitious.
- Prone to depression and anxiety.
- Low self-esteem.
- Overwhelming need to be nurtured, combined with a strong desire to help others.

My "mental coach" Seppo Heino conducted a lot of personality tests. Some of my results are typical of competitive athletes, such as the limitless ambition, which was literally off Heino's charts. I also had a fighter's attitude and absolute determination, which make all the difference in competitive sports. On the other hand, I had a lot of work to do on my self-esteem and raging anxiety. Even though I knew all this and tried my hardest to build a healthy mindset, in those years I had no clue how to manage these issues. In other words—and I'll admit it—some serious psychological issues were recognized early in my career but there weren't good strategies for dealing with them.

In any professional sport, the differences in raw physical capability are relatively small, a razor's edge. Emotional and mental resilience is what separates champions from the rest of the field. I knew this at a young age, and we wanted someone to help me develop these capacities. I began working with Seppo in 2006. He was a pioneer of the "mental game" long before it was a common term in sports. Among many other achievements, he had collaborated with the Finnish Olympic committee, and he had worked with the wonderful ice dance couple Susanna Rahkamo and Petri Kokko. So I thought he would be great.

Seppo taught me visualization and relaxation practices and helped me to structure my goals. He showed me how mental toughness was an indispensable part of the training regimen. His method allowed me to key into every moment in a performance: What are you thinking at this point in the program? How do you conceive this tough jump? Are you maintaining your concentration right to the last second and beyond? But first we had to backtrack and work on resilience, specifically how I dealt with failures and setbacks, which in figure skating take the form of the point tally, and the point tally depends to a large extent on jumps. It always comes down to those jumps! If you don't go into your jumps with a combination of courage and excellent technique, your score suffers. One of the most common problems is "popping" a jump, also known as settling for fewer rotations because you didn't have enough speed or the right launch timing. In Finnish, a popped jump is an *ilmapallo* (air balloon). Since my tendency was to rehearse a jump endlessly, I tended to become obsessed with perfection, and that worked against me. Our team agreed with Seppo that I would only try a particular jump two or three times in a row. If I popped a particular jump repeatedly, I had to move on to the next jump. Keep it moving.

This was a good strategy, but my mind was slippery. On the inside, I was not moving past the "failures." My thoughts chased each other in obsessive loops, repeating almost maniacally: "no *ilmapallo*; no *ilmapallo*." But this made me hesitant, so we switched up the strategy again and decided that a failed jump or outright fall was better than a popped jump, so, now, go for it, right? OK, fine, but I would lapse back into no *ilmapallo* because my thoughts refused to behave and made me hesitant at the takeoff. Seppo started introducing various visualization and relaxation exercises, bringing in music, working in complete silence, or experimenting with different mental images. I made some progress, but it didn't come easy and didn't seem to stick.

The issue was bigger than what happened or didn't happen on the ice. What was really hurting me was the lack of balance in my life. Skating crowded out many of the healthy things I should have been doing as a teenager. And it kept crowding things out. The further along my career went, the worse it got, to the point where my mood depended 100 percent on how things were going in my skating. If a training went badly, the whole day was ruined, and I mean dramatically destroyed, crushed, decimated. My social life was nonexistent. And as I said, my appearance, my body, and every scrap of food I ate—everything was filtered through my skating ambitions.

I tried to distract myself with games and hobbies, but either I got bored or I made a competition out of trying to have fun. I was very imperfect at trying not to be a perfectionist. At one point I asked for a PlayStation as a Christmas gift. I had read that world champion Javier Fernandez played a lot of PlayStation. But it wasn't my thing; it bored me silly. Seppo's well-meaning tricks and techniques frequently backfired, because I did them with that same fierce intensity I did skating itself. One time, Seppo said I should unwind by watching TV in my spare time and be as relaxed as possible, but I did it like someone takes medicine. I'd sit there watching, wondering, "Am I relaxed yet?" "When is this gonna work?" "Just one more show, come on, you can do it!"

> In sports there is a lot of talk about the pressures of publicity, but the internal pressures are much more critical. We dealt a lot with the issue of how Kiira could live a normal life without the pressure building to a crisis point. We dedicated huge amounts of time to it and tried to get Kiira to have a life—if I may say that. Kiira had almost no enrichment in her life that would have helped ease the pressure.—Seppo Heino, sports psychologist

Although Seppo and I did some beneficial work together, my anxiety remained high. I think his personality tests were interesting, but actually they made me even more self-conscious, and that led again to anxiety. I'm sure Seppo meant well, but his approach of trying to "fix me" and "get a life" for me was not helpful. It strengthened my belief that I was flawed and damaged.

My perfectionism seeped into everything. While working with Seppo, I wrote religiously in my training diary and gave each practice a grade from 1 to 5. A score of 1 meant the practice was bad and 5 was super good. I graded my mood on the same scale—every day. I loved to score everything, measure everything: the calories with every bite, total minutes spent sleeping, my weight in grams, the number of relaxation practices, and of course my jumps, always the jumps. How many? How well? What percentage landed? My days were filled with these calculations. They gave me a sense of security and control. But my diary from those days tells the real story; life was barely manageable:

> 1st of March 2008: *In the evening in the sauna I just felt like crying. I was so tired but at the same time so relieved about the week's training.*

> 5th of March 2008: *This morning I felt so depressed, but during the day my mood got better.*

> 16th of April 2008: *I don't know why I have this constant anxiety in my head. I would really like a hug from Susanna, not neglect.*

These diary entries, when I was 19 years old, already show the increasing pressure and stress.

I was constantly tired and I could have easily gone to bed at 7:30 and slept through the night. I wrote in my practice diary, almost daily, that I was tired, very tired, or extremely tired.

2nd of February 2008: *I'm so tired that there's no bottom to it.*

6th of March 2008: *On Saturday I just cried out of tiredness and relief. I have to fight through every practice.*

3rd of April 2008: *It was so hard to wake up from my nap, but I'm pushing hard, I'm fighting hard.*

Practicing became an all-out battle and a grueling performance. I would not dare to let myself even think I was tired (even though I constantly wrote it down in my diary) because that was a sign of weakness. I thought I just needed to keep on training and studying. I patted myself on the back for how wonderfully I kept on fighting, but in my off moments I knew I was in a dark place.

My mom says that she has never in her life seen someone as efficient as I was. If I ever had a rare day off, I had a big to-do list. I couldn't imagine a situation where I didn't have every hour of every day figured out. Years later, after my competitive career ended, one of the hardest adjustments was to not base my sense of self-worth on how much I do. Throughout my teens I would feel terrible about myself unless I'd met my goals of the day, of the week, and of the year, and I had heard some positive feedback about my progress. It has been and continues to be a learning curve to remember that I'm worthy of love for just being me no matter how little or how much I get done each day.

My parents wanted to raise hardworking and well-adjusted children. Who doesn't? Mom always reminded me how important it was to think about the needs and feelings of others. She says she tried so hard to keep my skating from dominating family life. It was a point of pride for her to say how "normal" life at the Korpi household was. But in all honesty, I think my mom's and our whole family's identity had become more and more attached to my skating success. I was predominantly a skater even at home whether my parents wanted to recognize that or not. Even when I was incredibly tired, and it became obvious that I had serious mental and physical challenges, I don't remember my parents ever questioning if all the training was healthy for me. They told me to keep pushing through, maybe believing it was good for me, and perhaps not wanting to sacrifice the uplift in our family's social status that came from my skating success.

Being ultra goal-oriented was the only way to live, I thought. I was all too proud of this. I imagined myself a better person because I had a clear mission, clear aims. Why didn't my sister Petra aim higher in her skating although she was in many ways more talented than I was? I couldn't understand why people didn't have greater ambitions. I even fell in love with my future husband partly because we shared the same driving ambition. Unlike most people I knew, though, I was ready to sacrifice my health and pretty much anything in order to reach my goals.

At practice, Maare and Susanna, meaning well, would work me hard, groom me for the big time, but when I did win, the message was—in more ways than one—get back to work, don't think too highly of yourself, be humble. Like Mom, they never quite allowed me to feel fully triumphant. Of course, everyone wanted me to succeed so badly, but when I did, it felt anticlimactic. Was that them, my culture, or just me? I began to feel that I didn't deserve all the attention and popularity, especially because it had come so suddenly. It was so confusing. My sponsors kept acting like I was the most important athlete in Finland, but deep inside I was deprived ... not of money, or fame, or medals, or external success of any kind ... but of unconditional love from the people I loved the most. I didn't realize all of this at the time.

I was a walking paradox. Instead of stepping back and saying, "Hey I need to reassess" or "I need to seek out people who are good for me," I put even more pressure on myself. If I'm feeling bad, sad, or nervous, then it must be my fault, right? And there's one way to fix it—*more practice*! Perfectionism and overworking were my ultimate defense mechanisms. If I could just be better at everything, and be an even better skater than I was, then the people I loved and respected would love and respect me back. Then, and only then, would I be happy. This was completely backward. The real Kiira was chasing the image of Kiira that was being manufactured for me, somewhere out there on magazine covers and in TV ads, and by Mom, and even by my team. Although no one ever said it out loud, I think I was expected to outperform both in school and at practice. All because I was *Kiira*, and Kiira had always performed so well at everything.

I noticed that Kiira was driving herself so hard at school, too. But she was already doing so well academically, and I thought she didn't need to be pushing herself so hard at school. But maybe Kiira got confused by my opinion.—Susanna Haarala, Kiira's coach, 2002–2013

The mental tiredness did start to show, and in morning practice I was especially nervous about what Kiira's mood would be that day.—Maaret Siromaa, Kiira's coach, 1996–2013

If anyone had said I was being a perfectionist, I would have denied it. After all, wasn't my room a total mess? Is this the room of a perfectionist? And then at school my average was only 9.9 out of 10. Not perfect. In my senior year in high school, I declined doing advanced studies in chemistry and physics. Not the actions of a perfectionist but of a profoundly lazy person, right? And then there were those other people who were so much better than me. I saw them, or thought I saw them, working more conscientiously, diligently, and effectively than I was.

Later in life I was fortunate to meet Satu (my mental coach after Seppo) and others who have provided safe spaces for me to be who I am. They didn't and don't try to fix me: they see me, hear me and meet me where I am. They emanate kindness, acceptance and compassion. They don't try to make my fears and doubts disappear; they create space for those uncomfortable feelings to emerge, and together—in safety and love—we can face them and let go of them. It has been a long road back to this simple and powerful ethic of care. I can't think of a more precious gift any person can give to another person than the gift of serving as an honest mirror of your inborn goodness and uniqueness that you yourself might have forgotten. *That* is what I now strive to be for others whenever I can.

⇒ 12 ⇐

The Big Fall

Kiira was always very earnest and that led to sky-high expectations. I hoped that if she could relax a bit more, it might reflect on the ice. It was a pursuit of perfection, which, on the other hand, was the reason why Kiira got so far.—Arthur Borges, Kiira's husband

To be honest, my perfectionism produced results, at least for a while. At the same time, considering my mental state and level of maturity, every setback was torture:

26th of January 2008: *I'm so pissed about missing a medal. But I need to just be happy for Lare [Laura Lepistö], and keep my own goals in mind. At least now I know exactly what to improve on when I go for the World Championships.*

20th of March 2008: *I feel absolutely awful after the competition. The difference in training and courage really showed. I'm not ready to join the elite group!*

During that difficult 2008 season, I wrote often in my diary about disappointment, anger, and regret, but I hung tough, and at both the European and worlds I placed well after my short program. My coaches kept working on my mental game. Together with Maare and Susanna we came up with a series of mantras to help me keep my thoughts together during competition performances. At the Europeans Maare came up with a phrase I liked: "I want, therefore I can." That took me through the short program, but once I was in the free program, I hit a wall. It was difficult for me to skate two good programs in the same competition, which was unfortunately a challenge throughout my career.

Commentators started calling me a short-program skater. They can be so annoying! But I can understand why they'd say that. I believe one reason was my physical condition, which wasn't on par with the world's best, probably due in large part to my eating disorder(s). In the four-minute free programs I found myself at my absolute limit. My coaches scrambled to help me stay steady.

Being rinkside was nerve wracking for me as coach. I wanted to be very careful with my words so I wouldn't upset Kiira, but perhaps I was too careful. Sometimes I felt I should have come up with something better to brace Kiira before crucial programs.—Maaret Siromaa, Kiira's coach, 1996–2013

My free program at the world championships in Göteborg 2008 was pathetic—almost everything went wrong. A triple toe loop with my hand touching down on the ice, a popped Lutz, and a fall in the middle of a spiral sequence. This wasn't supposed to happen. My self-esteem was shattered even if my final standings weren't all that bad. I was in 17th place in the free skating portion and with my points from the short program I was 9th overall. This remains my best result at the world championships, even if I was full of gloom and regret back then.

My mind was betraying me. I was my own worst enemy. Somewhere along the way I lost a sense of ease and confidence. When I was younger, I thought of myself as the competitive and winning type, but at some point, I stopped seeing myself as a winner. Still, amazingly, I kept winning even while my emotions were all over the place. A deep sense of insecurity was eating me up in Göteborg. I didn't believe I belonged with the best skaters in the world, and I didn't see myself as good enough to skate with the final six skaters at the world championships. Carolina Kostner, Mao Asada, Yukari Nakano, Joannie Rochette, Yuna Kim, and me. World champions, Olympic medalists, and me. No way. And yet I still had finished fourth in the short program in such a strong crowd!

After my terrible free program in Göteborg, I wanted so badly to hide, to avoid the public, to not answer a single question, or even see my friends. I was embarrassed, ashamed, sad, and wanted to cry all the time. I cried so much that the mixture of tears and competition make-up gave me a rash on my cheeks. My mind was always racing. I felt like I had failed everyone, my sponsors, my coaches, my family, and all of Finland. Heavy load for a 19-year-old! In reality there was a lot of warmth and compassion coming my way, but I interpreted it as pity. It was like being in a trance, and I wished I could snap out of it. It took weeks to get past these feelings and be able to think clearly again.

The career of a figure skater is long, and failure can happen many times. So it's essential to have a strategy to deal with this effectively. In Finland, I think we could do better. Right now, I would argue that if an athlete fails twice in an important major competition in their peak years, there won't be a third competition if the failures aren't dealt with thoroughly.—Seppo Heino, sports psychologist

After Göteborg, I flew to the invitation-only competition in Japan in May 2008, took the university entrance exams and started prepping for the next skating season.

People in Finland had been eagerly awaiting 2008–2009 for years because we were going to host the European championships in Helsinki! I was looking forward to this competition so much. But then my condition started to slip, and the mysterious leg problems began. My coaches and I had to face the terrible possibility that I might miss the Helsinki Europeans, even as Valio was making me one of the faces of the upcoming event—as if there wasn't enough pressure!

There was a ray of hope, though. My physiotherapist Jarmo "Jami" Ahonen continued to work his magic on my legs, and they were getting stronger. Would it be enough? After I skipped a big chunk of the fall and winter competitions, my first appearance was at the Finnish championships in December 2008, just a month before the European championships. My competitors already had two to three months under their belts, but to everyone's surprise, including mine, I left Laura and Susanna Pöykiö behind and won my first Finnish championship. There would be four more in my career!

I had a Finnish gold medal, but the chopped-up season was bound to catch up with me, right? There I was, at the European championships, Hartwell Arena, Helsinki, with "home court advantage," as they say in the States. I was in the final group of six, but I had struggled with my opening Lutz in the six-minute warm-up, and the jump didn't go well in the actual program either. I had to throw both hands on the ice to keep myself from falling altogether and then of course missed the double toe loop that was supposed to follow it. Then, the judges scored the landing of my triple loop as incomplete, which cost me more points. I disputed it—something I rarely did—because for me the jump felt completely clean (I later saw from a video that the judges had been right). After the short program I was seventh and Laura and Sussu were the top two. Then came free skating. That day, the 24th of January 2009, has become part of Finnish figure skating history.

The arena was completely full of people and full of Finnish flags. Tappara flags, too. The medal expectations of the Finnish audience were sky high after the short program. Laura and Sussu were in great shape in the standings, and I was only four points out of third place. If I could skate a good free program, it was possible for me to medal. I took my opening position, did my first easy steps, and picked up speed with backward crossovers, just as I had done tens of thousands of times before. All of a sudden everything got crazy.

As if in a slow-motion video, I fell down on my third crossover in the first seconds of my free program and glided to the side of the rink in front of the fully packed home arena. Instead of fighting for a medal I found myself flat on the ice. My first thought was whether I had been seriously injured. I had landed so hard, and my lower back was sore. My emotions went from one extreme to another: I was shocked, embarrassed. How can this be happening? How many point deductions will I get? Should I even keep skating? I had never before tripped in these crossovers; it was a complete rookie mistake. But somehow, I got myself up and coasted over to Maare. I was badly shaken. She was perfectly calm or seemed to be, anyway. She said, "Are you hurt? Can you go on? I know you can. Kiira, you have three minutes. Three minutes, there is no problem, no rush. Now just breathe, breathe, and we start over."

The fall at the European championships in Helsinki, 2009 (photograph by Grigory Dukor, Lehtikuva / Reuters / Grigory Dukor).

12. The Big Fall

Do I start from the beginning or from where I left off? I breathed in short gulps and listened like I'd never listened before. Through the haze of my mind and the noise of the crowd, I head Maare repeating how I had three whole minutes left. Someone gripped my hand tightly. Maare herself was drowned in a wave of emotions, as she later told me, but her inner coach took over and she knew exactly the right thing to say right then. The music started again, and I picked up where I had left off. The first Lutz failed again, but the rest of the program went OK. No, it went more than OK. The audience came to my rescue.

I don't know what would have happened if it hadn't been for the 10,000 Finns who got me through those last two minutes. I saw all the Tappara and Finnish flags and I just knew they truly wanted me to succeed. I skated my heart out. Eventually I placed fifth, a miracle! This was by far the most replayed fall of my career. Those European championships in Finland are remembered for three things: Laura's gold, Sussu's bronze, and my tumble. Years later, I was asked at a sports gala what I thought was the most memorable moment of my career. I knew right away. Not the medals, not Torino or the early successes, but falling, falling in the European championships on home ice and how the fans got me back on my feet and across the finish line.

≈ 13 ≈

Friendship and Envy

In summer 2009, months after my "big fall," I traveled to Vancouver with my dear friend Laura Lepistö and Susanna Pöykiö to prepare for the 2010 Winter Olympics the following February. We knew that at some point in the coming months, one of us would be very sad. Finland would send only two figure skaters to the Vancouver Winter Olympics.

There was a lot of excitement in the air. We three were at the forefront of Finnish skating. In the past four seasons we had netted five European championship medals between us, and the Finnish Olympic Committee was taking more and more notice of our sport. More notice meant more support. The committee provided funds for our personal coaches to join us at the three-week camp in Vancouver. It was a unique chance for us to work together in the summer, and we were pumped. We also became closer as a national team. We had to because they put us all in the same rented house (but that had some downsides, too!).

Over the years, I had become used to rooming with Laura—no stress, no fuss. We had known each other since we were 11, and we had plenty in common. It was always great to go to the camps if Laura was there, and we got to know each other during those summers away from Finland. It was also so impressive to see her get stronger and more skillful. We were goods friends and pushed each other to get better. If Laura landed a brilliant jump, I'd find myself landing that same jump not too long afterward and vice versa. In the past, the top Finnish women skaters had a reputation for feuding. I'll bet many fans wondered why Laura and I cheered each other on. And why were our coaches so nice to each other? I don't know the answer myself! But I do know that all the positive energy flowing between Laura and me made us better skaters. I also know that once we entered the arena, we became fierce, game faces on, going all out for the win. That felt good, too.

This group won altogether nine championship medals for Finland. In summer 2009, we trained in Vancouver where the Olympics were held the next year. From left: me, Susanna Pöykiö, Laura Lepistö, Heidi Pöykiö, Susanna Haarala, Maaret Siromaa, and Virpi Horttana.

Laura and I never demanded special perks at the camps. We probably should have! Looking back I wish I had asked for two important additions to our international team, a doctor and a physical therapist. The American skaters usually had them and a masseuse, too! So did the Italians and pretty much all the other major skating countries. I started hiring my own physical therapist. For the Vancouver season the federation finally provided us with the talented physiotherapist Lilli Helpi, who toured with us to a number of competitions.

It took me a while to be comfortable making demands. Sussu, on the other hand, was not the least bit shy about asking for exactly what she wanted. I saw that in Vancouver. I soon found out it was challenging to board with her. The second she arrived, Sussu declared she was taking the biggest bedroom in the house. Laura and I squeezed into a smaller bedroom where we shared a narrow bed. If Sussu wanted to eat fish, we all ate fish. If the training routine wasn't to her liking, she did a different routine. Annoying, but, then again, there was something refreshing about someone who was so up front about what she wanted. Maybe I should have had the courage to ask loudly for what I wanted, too, and the courage to talk back to Sussu. Instead, Laura and I went along with everything and did our whining behind her back. At the end of the day, though, we're talking about minor stuff here. Sussu was still my inspiration, and most of the time, we got along really well.

I felt for her. Sussu was six years older than me and Laura, and I imagine she was feeling the pressure of expectations for what would likely be her last Olympics. It turned out that she would not qualify that year. The two Olympic spots for solo Finnish skaters would be determined in January 2010 at the European championships in Tallinn. After her short program, Sussu was 20 points behind Laura and me. She withdrew from the competition before her free program, and so concluded the magnificent career of a Finnish pioneer. Sussu's success and rise to the position of the first Finnish woman to win an international championship medal will always be a beacon for all Finnish athletes.

When Sussu faltered in Tallinn, the Olympic picks were set. Laura snared the European championship silver, and I was fourth. We two would represent Finland! I was so happy because Vancouver would probably be my best Olympic opportunity. Torino had been too early, and Sochi was a possibility, but I might be too old then. In Vancouver I would be in good physical shape at the age of 21. Moreover, I had been consistently healthy, something that was becoming rare for me, and most important, I was working on some new and more difficult programs. The stars seemed aligned for me to do really well in Vancouver, and then bam! In 22 seconds my dream was crushed.

Twenty-two seconds into my short program. That's when I crashed into the side of the rink, right in front of the Olympic rings. My triple Lutz was under-rotated, and I landed on a completely straight leg and fell with all my weight onto my left buttock. I thought I'd torn my glutes, the pain was crazy, but of course I got up and kept going. No way would I give up just like that, but the points I would have gotten from this crucial jump combination were now out of reach. Just like that my hopes of making it into the top five were destroyed. The resulting score was 12 points lower than my short program at the Europeans just one month earlier, the best short program of my career. This was one of the biggest disappointments I ever experienced, but then the free program that followed was one of my best! I placed 11th overall at the Olympics.

13. Friendship and Envy

A bittersweet result, but my coach Susanna was there to put it in perspective: "You are a fighter. This is a moment you should savor."

I wasn't sure if I *could* savor it, but in the end, it was a huge relief that the incredible pressure of the Olympics was now behind me. And Laura! She made Finnish Olympic history as the highest ranked Finn ever, sixth place overall.

Now we would get some rest and a breather from practicing, and we could finally enjoy the Olympic atmosphere. Or so we thought. Our coaches came up with the brilliant plan of reserving ice time for additional practice a few days after our competition. They wanted us to start preparing for the world championships right away. Figure skating is one of the only Olympic sports where the European and world championships take place every year, even in Olympic years. That means that athletes in our sport typically perform in three major events in a row. Long story short, there was less than a month until the worlds, and according to the coaches, we would benefit by practicing at the Olympic Village before our journey home. It felt cruel and unreasonable because Laura and I had left it all on the ice. Now we were expected to hit the rink first thing in the morning. Then there was the small fact that certain Finnish hockey stars had invited us to go out to party.

"Text your coaches that you're skipping the training. Come celebrate with us!"

Laura and I wondered what to do.

We were too conscientious to skip practice, but we did want to enjoy our time at the Olympics. When the limos pulled up, we jumped in. That night, we had a great time with our fellow athletes. Our tables were loaded with drinks and junk food. The check was not a problem as some big shot hockey execs took care of it. This was nothing for them. They had bought brand new flat screen TVs for every member of the national hockey team to put in their very basic lodgings. When the Winter Games were over, the TVs were given to some of the volunteers who came to work at the Olympic Village.

I have good memories of that night. I even had a couple of drinks, very unusual for me. In the morning I dutifully showed up for practice, but it was like skating uphill for the first half hour. That was the only time in my career that I have ever been on the ice with a hangover, not to mention how exhausted I was from the run-up to Vancouver. Our coaches weren't clued into all that, or at least they didn't let on if they were. The practice was as rigorous as always. They were dead set on getting us ready for the next competition.

It's not only skaters who make it a point of honor to work extra hard and eat extra carefully. We were constantly comparing ourselves to each other, silently competing all the time. Lots of side eye at meals and at practice. But our coaches also loved showing off to each other. It was all about who works their skaters harder. That's my theory, anyway. Soon I pushed all signs of fatigue aside and got into the full swing of practice in the Olympic Village, already looking forward hungrily to the next challenge. My ambition in those days was limitless (=obsessive). My diary tells the tale:

8th of August 2010: *Next season, same level as Laura or at least close to it. The year after that, overtake Laura and be the best in Finland.*

Honestly, I envied Laura and I was saddened by not winning medals. She seemed to have success after success. At the world championships in Torino, she won a bronze and was the number one Finnish female in the competition. This was historic for Finland, our first and, as of the publication of this book, still our only world championship medal in individual figure skating. For me the competition was a flop; I came in 19th. If I had been true to myself and not been in denial about my overwhelming exhaustion, I would have skipped it altogether. I should have given my spot to someone else.

Laura hogged four medals in major international competitions between 2008 and 2010, and I didn't get one. I was surely happy for her, but I also badly wanted to be ranked higher than her. I'd write down our competition scores and exactly how many points separated us. Laura beat me at every competition in 2009–2010. The smallest difference was one point something and the widest spread was 40 points. I made a plan of how I would first narrow our averages and then eventually become number one in Finland. I planned this to happen at the latest in the 2011–2012 season. This fixation wormed its way into my mind. Number one. Best in Finland. It would be tragic if it didn't happen.

14

The Man with
the Strange Name

Villa del Balbianello sits on a hill that rises up out of the forest along the shores of Lake Como. From its gardens you can see Lake Como shimmering in its many shades of blue, a sight thousands come to enjoy every year. The Franciscans really knew where to put a monastery. The walls of the stone house, built in the 13th century, have witnessed the prayers of monks and cardinals, the decisions of political leaders, the creative struggles of great writers, and the incredible tales of explorers. This is where he brought me. We laughed, we joked, we loved.

What about love? I was in my early 20s and alone. I was convinced I would never meet anyone in Finland. I spent all my time either in school or at the rink. There, the options were limited to ice hockey players and Zamboni drivers, and at school no one approached me. Was it me? Don't know. In college I went out with one boy, and I was the one who asked him out. That didn't last. I was longing for a serious relationship.

I always imagined that I would end up with an athlete. As a teenager I dated Sami, who played ice hockey for Ilves. At one of the summer camps I had a short romance with an American skater named Pierre, and once I went on a dinner date in Näsinneula with a certain Sebastian. He was moving up in motorsports and was looking for a summer house in Finland. Then there was the snowboarder at the Torino Winter Olympics, a good guy. Janne and I were in a relationship for about a year and a half. We both lived the lives of professional athletes, which meant we saw each other very little. Janne is a lovely man, and we are still friends, but a relationship with him wasn't right for me.

Eventually I found who *was* right for me, of course by chance. I was at a charity ice show in March of 2010, and I spotted the famous singer Anna Abreu. We were both there to perform to raise funds for girls and women in developing countries. She noticed me and headed over to where I was.

"Hey, Kiira, are you still with that snowboarder?"

"No. It's been over for a year now."

"Good. I have the perfect man for you."

Anna took out her phone and showed me pictures of a man on her Facebook page. He had an unusual name for a Finn, Arthur Borges. The man was friends with Anna's boyfriend at the time, Joonas. They had all had dinner together the night before. That Borges guy joked that Anna should ask me out for him, and Anna had taken him literally. The man with the weird name lived in Milan, worked in fashion, and had done some modeling, too. Didn't sound like my type at all.

"Here's Arthur's number, call him. Yes, yes. Yes? Go ahead and call him!"

I took the number from Anna just to be polite. There was *no way* I was going to call him. What would I have said? Hi, I'm Kiira, wanna hang out? Nope. About a week after the ice gala I decided to friend him on Facebook—no harm in that, right? I was surprised to find out that we had a few things in common. OK, he seems like a nice guy, I thought. The world championships in Torino were going to be in a couple of days. I asked Arthur to come and see the competition. It was only about an hour's drive from Milan to Torino.

Arthur made the drive and bought black market tickets for 200 euros, but they were in the nosebleed section. He sat there by himself and watched figure skating live for the first time in his life. He didn't know much about my sport. Maybe that was a good thing, as my competition was a complete failure.

We saw each other outside the arena afterward, but it was hard to connect. I was surrounded by a large group of kids wanting autographs. After that I had to rush out to dinner with Mikko's manager friends. Arthur asked if we could see each other afterward. He said he could wait at a friend's place until I was free. Arthur actually didn't have any friends in Torino. He just sat in his car in a parking lot, with the driver's seat pushed all the way back, waiting for my text. The dinner went on and on and it was getting close to midnight. He was about to drive back to Milan, but then I texted him just in time to say that the dinner was almost over.

A tall, impressive-looking man with thick, dark hair walked into the restaurant. Our conversation started innocently, but it's hard to put into words the way his voice made me feel. All I can say is that I liked his simple, direct style.

"Hi, what would you like to drink?"

"I don't really know."

"Good. I'll order you something nice. So you're a figure skater? I think I might have heard about you at some point."

We talked through the night. Arthur was born in the Canary Islands. His mom is Finnish and dad Spanish, which explained the non–Finnish surname. Arthur had moved to Porvoo when he was eight years old and went on to study fashion in Germany and Madrid. He worked as a model in Milan and then became the Baltic and Nordic regional manager for Armani. We had very similar values. We were both very ambitious, but we cherished our connections to family and friends. We also discovered that I knew as little about the fashion industry as Arthur did about figure skating. We would have a lot to share.

What can I say? It was love. I knew right away that something special was beginning. In the morning I needed to hide my silly grin. I didn't want Maare to wonder why I was looking so happy after such a crappy competition.

Lonely clouds glide in the blue sky and invite the sun to play with light and shadow. The thunderstorm the evening before has cleared the skies completely. I sit on a boat with my maids of honor and we're being waited on. I'm smiling so much that my cheeks are hurting. The snowy peaks are magically framing the view. I ask Petra, "Is this real?" Our boat softly touches shore, and at a distance I see the paparazzi in their boat pointing their cameras at me. Typically I would be annoyed but now I'm so happy that I just grin toward the cameras. I start to climb the stairs carefully but impatiently. I try to navigate the ancient stone steps in the gorgeous wedding gown Teemu designed for me. At the top Dad is already waiting and he looks nervous. Everything is ready. When I hear the clear tones of the harp and violin start up, the emotions rush through me. I squeeze Dad's hand hard and fight back tears. There's Arthur at the end of the aisle, and with each step I'm closer to him. When I arrive beside him, he takes my hand and whispers in my ear: "I have never seen anything so beautiful."

The first five years of our relationship we lived apart, usually in different countries, and we had completely packed schedules. We did manage to see each other a lot though. Usually I was the one who traveled to where he was, and that usually meant Milano. The long weekends together in that elegant Italian city were a lovely break from practice. Long-distance relationships are not easy but I'm actually glad we didn't live together in the early days. Arthur would probably have gotten fed up with my uptightness, which showed up in more ways than one. When we first hugged, Arthur declared that I had a "rock-hard back." Did he mean I was muscular or that I was tense? Probably both.

> In the beginning it was difficult for me to understand why Kiira was always thinking about her career. Skating and the goals that go with it were the most important things in her life and I sometimes felt I was second. If we had lived together while she was still competing, it would have been tough. —Arthur Borges, Kiira's husband

Arthur was so much more relaxed than I was at that time. He was open and warm, and he got excited about every new thing. In many ways he is like his mother Rauna, who is the picture of positive thinking.

Arthur shook up my attitude toward life and toward skating, and that was a very good thing. He didn't have much patience to listen to my endless complaints about my profession. Sometimes he would interrupt my rants by saying, "What are you stressing about?" "Why do you bother your mind with something like that?" I would sometimes get angry because I thought he didn't understand me, didn't empathize with me. But afterward I realized he was probably right.

With Arthur at Lago Maggiore, 2018.

14. The Man with the Strange Name

As time went by, I became more and more relaxed around him, and he showed me how important it is to let loose sometimes and to admit to yourself what you really want. If we bought three bottles of wine, my instinct would be to open the cheapest one and save the better bottles for later. Arthur will always reach for the most expensive one first, because if not now, then when? Exactly.

> Kiira was shy about making her personal goals and dreams known to others. She had for some reason been taught to repeat to herself that she is just an ordinary girl. I wanted to convince her that she is anything but an ordinary girl and that she was doing extraordinary things.—Arthur Borges, Kiira's husband

I shared so much with Arthur, but I also absolutely insisted that our relationship and my life not be talked about publicly. I had learned to never comment on my private life to the media, a rule I stuck to throughout my competitive career. That meant, though, that if rumors started in the media, we didn't attempt to correct them, which led to some funny situations.

Some reporter found out that Arthur had worked as a model in Italy. Then there was his exotic name, at least for Finns, and immediately a rumor started that I was in a relationship with an Italian model. It sounded media sexy. At the Finnish presidential reception in 2015, about half of the guests started a conversation with Arthur in English, not knowing he was a native Finn. Actually, my "Italian model" boyfriend was a specialist in made-to-measure suits at Tom Ford and sold suits worth tens of thousands to clients all around the world. To the Finnish media he was an Italian model, but we just let them think what they thought. We never gave interviews and did not go to public events together. Only after my competitive career was over did we become much more relaxed about our public activities. But now, back to that magical day:

> *Feeling grateful and happy. Not only about him but about the love we are sharing with friends and family. I'm glad I didn't give in to my impulse to keep the wedding small and economical (a trait I inherited from my dad). Instead we put together an unforgettable experience that we got to share with all the people close to us. Family, friends, and skating buddies in Finland and around the world. A magical event in a magical atmosphere. The memories are still fresh: Dad's and Rauna's speeches, Eeva-Mummi's poem, Petra's lovely words, Maria's touching rendition of "Over the Rainbow," Maare and Susanna's emotional words, Mom's forever hug, Jare's and Kimmo's*

performances, and Arthur's song choice for me: "Pakko saada sut" (I Have to Have You) performed by Petra's husband Markku and his rap buddies. Everything was perfect. I lived every moment thoroughly and I was soaking in all the caring and love. It was downright soul healing.

Our wedding in Italy, 2015.

≈ 15 ≈

Police Costume

Up until the Olympic season of 2009–2010 I thought that I didn't need a famous (or expensive) choreographer. Figure skating is not figure skating without the music, the outfits, the drama, and, at the heart of the experience, the choreography. All these things together are what makes the sport so beloved among fans. I knew all this, but it took me a really long time to think seriously about getting a world-class choreographer to work on my programs. I think I tried to convince myself that my original team was "good enough," or maybe I didn't believe I needed or deserved a world-class choreographer even if I was already a world-class skater. Also, I was more in my comfort zone with people I knew. My heart knew the score as usual. It was whispering to me to "go and be big" in every way I could.

Nelli Petänen had designed my first program in Tampere when I was 13 years old, and we continued working in a comfortable way for a long time. In between seasons, Nelli would come to our practices with well-thought-out choreography, and we would have the basic moves in place in two or three sessions. It was easy and efficient, leaving a lot of time for technical and physical training. We would weigh different musical options with Nelli and the coaches. Sometimes I would bring in music that I absolutely had to skate to—I had such deep longings for certain music. This was how I felt about one of my 2008 free skate tracks, "Agatha," by Kerkko Koskinen, which I first heard on a flight from Japan to Finland.

Skating choreography is so much more than picking a musical number and deciding on a sequence of tricks to do on the ice to go along with it. The choreographer has to follow very strict rules about the number and category of technical elements. In a short program, for instance, there needs to be three jumps minimum, one of which must be an axel and one a jump combination. The short program must also include three different spins and a step sequence. Working within these guidelines, the choreographer then has to do the hard work of creating a program that is complete, seamless, and beautiful. This is a process. First, the choreographer seeks out a theme and music that would suit the skater as an individual and then thinks through every transition, makes sure that the movements cover the whole rink, and comes up with original moves and gestures that we hope will catch the eye of the audience and the judges. To integrate the step sequence in a competition program, choreographers spend many hours on and off the ice to come up with innovative step and turn patterns. Considering all this, it's only right that choreography and composition are factored into the final score. Good choreography makes a program into a work of art.

I had been happy with Nelli's programs, and our collaboration had lasted for almost ten years. But after the Olympic season of 2009–2010, I wanted new winds to blow through my performances. I had outgrown Nelli's programs, and I realized that my choreography wasn't at the highest possible level. Actually, many people thought I should have gone with new choreographers much earlier, but only after Vancouver was I mentally ready to leave my comfort zone.

I now had the financial means to invest in the best. My coaches Susanna and Maare supported the decision. Susanna Pöykiö had gone with the great Canadian choreographer Lori Nichol, and Sussu's example encouraged me once again. My manager Mikko had gotten to know the Canadian David Wilson while I was in Korea performing in Yuna Kim's show. David was Yuna's choreographer and probably the most sought-after skating choreographer at that time. His own skating career had ended early with a knee injury but now, at age 50, he was a very successful program creator. His accomplishments included choreographies that have won world championships and Olympic medals. I wanted to work with the best, and so Mikko approached David and asked if he could create a new program for me. I knew that work requests were pouring in for David. In the course of a season he could pick only a few of the most interesting assignments.

"I thought you'd never ask," said David. "Of course I'll do it."

David would undertake the all-important free program. I badly needed to retool this part of my skating. Should I go for a complete overhaul, though? I usually reworked one program per season, but then I thought, "Why not go for a new short program, too?" Figure skaters usually have different choreographers for their two programs, so I asked

15. Police Costume

David to recommend someone. He suggested Shae-Lynn Bourne, also a Canadian. Shae-Lynn (Shae) and her partner Victor Kraatz had won the 2003 world championship for ice dancing. She began designing programs in 2006. Excited, I traveled to Canada in the summer of 2010 to learn my new material.

People back in Finland were stunned at the price tag, especially compared to what we'd paid back in Tampere. Nelli's programs would usually cost me about 350 euros, but in Canada, this number would have at least one extra zero. David might charge over 15 fold compared to Finnish price level for a short program of a little over two minutes. Shae-Lynn was not as well-known, but as she gained positive reviews, she commanded higher and higher sums. Working with these choreographers was new in other ways, too. Whereas with Nelli we could finalize a program with a couple of ice practices, David might take a whole day to just get a feel for the music.

Even though David didn't always step on the ice in his skates, he had a very strong vision of the program and how it should go. He was super detail-oriented, and we might fine tune the direction of a glance and the position of a head to within millimeters. David was masterful in customizing themes, choosing the right music and "look" for each individual skater, adapting to that skater's strengths. For me, he created a free program with music from *Evita* in collaboration with the talented Hugo Chouinard, a master of creating program music that matches the rhythm of the skater's movements. Stuttering, scratchy, or fragmented musical accompaniment is horrible to listen to. For my *Evita* program, Hugo created a complex track blending eight songs, seamless, smooth, and eloquent.

David is brilliant, a genius, but he was also temperamental. It wasn't unusual for him to come to practice late. Sometimes he mixed up the days of the week. I was never sure what mood he'd be in. There'd be tears streaming down his cheeks when he heard the music. A single hand movement during my routine might make him ecstatic or make him upset.

A few years after we first started working together, we decided to do a show program. A show program can be plugged into a commercial skating show and can also be useful when you're asked to perform at one of the closing events at international competitions. There is often a gala after championship week. Choreography for a show program is more fanciful because there aren't many rules or restrictions.

It can include playful combinations of set pieces, costumes, and dance styles, all designed to delight the audience. I remember "Sex Bomb," a show piece with Russian skater Evgeni Plushenko. He came out looking like a body builder and did a series of very raunchy moves. Then there were Surya Bonaly's shows with those amazing back flips.

During our work on the show piece, there was a big blow up that took me by surprise. I had been working with David for a while and I thought we knew each other well. At one point in our review of my moves I complained to David about one little detail.

"This one spiral doesn't feel right for me. I don't want to do it here," I said.

David exploded: "Goddammit, you are like a 13-year-old. I can't deal with this!"

He stomped off, slamming doors as he went. You could hear the echoes all through the rink. He broke the door of the changing room and the other skaters stopped and stared. Arthur happened to be there too, and he looked on in wonder. I didn't think I had been rude at all, although maybe the way I phrased my comment was annoying. On the other hand, David did have a tendency to occasionally lose his cool with skaters that he worked closely with.

I thought about what could have set him off. Maybe the elephant in the room was that I had ordered *both* my competition programs that season from Shae-Lynn. This might have hurt David's feelings. I thought I needed to keep David happy, and I had asked him to plan the show program. This was typical for me. I wanted to smooth over any possible conflict. It's a weakness of mine, and I've learned that if you're not making a gesture for the right reasons, from the heart, people will resent it. Things ended amicably, though, as it didn't take too long for us to apologize to each other. I love David.

Then there was Shae, my friend Shae. She always came to the arena with good energy. You could feel it from far away. It was empowering. She is an exceptionally skilled figure skater and did a lot of skating during our sessions. I remember thinking how I could be this clumsy on skates compared to her, although I was already ranked among the world's best skaters! Shae was able to do anything on ice and in any way. I was envious of her but also extremely inspired watching her, and as time went on, we became good friends.

When I first met Kiira, I thought she was trying to be too precise and perfect, which made her skating stiff. The transformation was wonderful when

15. *Police Costume*

Kiira gave herself permission to be more free. When her skating became more fluid, her beautiful body language could shine through.—Shae-Lynn Bourne, choreographer

Shae liked to make up and practice different sequences of movements. We skated hours on end, trying hundreds of variations. Shae always asked what felt the most natural for me. What did she mean by "natural"? Before I met Shae, I believed that a particular move doesn't have to feel natural at first but should be practiced and practiced until it works. But with Shae I learned to sense the signals my body was sending me, its unique way of moving. This helped me see my skating more and more as a form of artistic expression.

Music was at the center of everything for Shae. Earlier with Nelli and my coaches we had tried to include difficult transitions including counter and rocker steps in the programs so that the transitions component would generate as high a score as possible. In contrast, Shae didn't believe in adding any movement to the choreography that didn't fit in perfectly with the music. If she felt that just a simple glide worked better than a complicated step, the glide was added to the program. Shae's "natural" approach became the organizing concept behind my programs.

Shae is one of the people who has left the biggest positive mark in my life, whose whole way of working I admire the most. There is freedom and joy in everything she does and the way she *is*. I remember a moment with her that left a huge impression on me. We were practicing my short program at a rink in Toronto. The world championships were coming up, the program was ready, and we were just fine tuning. I popped the first triple-triple combination, which annoyed me so much that I just stopped skating—a definite no-no. Then Shae asked calmly if I'd like to start again. I did, and the same thing happened with the combo. I stopped *again*. I was getting really angry at myself for messing up this important practice. I skated to the boards where Shae was, looking calm as could be. She was standing there with a beautiful posture and a gentle look on her face, and she said, "It's OK, Kiira, one more time now?" Behind those simple words were all the hours of advice, teamwork, creative moments, and tips on how to respect and listen to my body. Those words sparked me, brought back all the good stuff in my relationship with Shae.

I'd never worked with anyone so calm and composed. To stop your program in the middle is unheard of in final practices. You must keep going. Unless you really hurt yourself, coaches won't allow you to stop even if you fail at every single element. If you do stop and lose your cool, your coach will let you know how disappointed they are in you. Coaches might also get sucked into the skater's state of mind and start spewing emotions—definitely not a good strategy. But Shae witnessed my little tantrum on the ice and remained centered in her own power. It was a transformative experience for me.

When I skated the program a third time it was clean and beautiful. I have often thought about that day. It was such a simple thing Shae did but so different from what I was used to. When I did something wrong, I expected shouting or stern words or critical looks. I couldn't believe that a coach or choreographer could relate to a skater's struggles in that gentle and powerful way. Nowadays, when I work with skaters, I try to remember everything I learned from Shae—to stay centered and grounded in my own power and provide space for the young person or adult student to be human, to have their feelings.

> I remember when Kiira came to Tampere from Canada after the summer. We coaches got to see the program for the first time and we both cried. Her practice style had also been transformed so that the program itself was the priority. Everything was polished to the finest detail including facial expressions that Kiira had mastered even in practice. In Canada Kiira learned that the feeling and expression of choreography was part of the whole discipline of skating.—Susanna Haarala, Kiira's coach, 2002–2013

By 2015, David and Shae had designed a total of six programs for me, and with those programs I won two European championship medals, two Grand Prix competitions and five Finnish championships. Those successes would not have been possible without the best choreographers in the world. Understanding the irreplaceable work of these two choreographers has given me the courage to design programs for young skaters now that my competitive career is over. I follow the core principles I learned from David and Shae. We come to the ice with a keen sensitivity to the music. Sequences and patterns or the step sequence are sketched out before we get to rehearsal, but only when we try them on the ice do we know if something really works or not. We feel our unique bodies responding, to the music, to the weight on our legs, to the way the cool air moves across our face, and then building on these feelings and sensations we skate on and on.

Another choreographer I worked with was maybe even better known than David or Shae-Lynn. In December 2009 I started on a new show program with Marvin Smith. I was introduced by Oliver Höner, the director of the Art on Ice show in Switzerland. Oliver wanted to get me to perform at one of his shows. Oliver had been manager to Sarah Meier and Stéphane Lambiel, and I got to know him via Mikko. After he put me in touch with Marvin, we flew him over from New York to Helsinki in business class so he could create a three-minute show number for me. Things went well with Marvin, but I still wasn't comfortable doing the Art on Ice show as it would have messed up my practice routine. Oliver got so upset about this that he threatened to blackball me from all of his shows indefinitely. I stuck to my guns, but so did Oliver. For years I didn't receive any invites to his shows, until in 2013, when I skated at the Art on Ice show in Helsinki.

Marvin's idea for the show number was inspired by Beyoncé's "If I Were a Boy" video where she dresses up as a police officer. My outfit in Marvin's program was a dark blue police costume. The seams and pockets were bordered with sparkling crystals. I wore skintight leggings. A police hat hid my ponytail. Hanging from my waist were handcuffs and a holster—fake, obviously. Underneath I was wearing an all-black skating outfit that was revealed once I tore off the police costume halfway through the program. It didn't cross my mind what kind of reactions I'd get. I was very naive. When I walked the hallways of the Saku Arena in Tallinn in that costume, the other show skaters from the European championships started to whistle and shout. That's when I realized my police routine would get a lot of attention. The night before I had cried in disappointment when I finished fourth, a mere .86 points out of the medals, but the next day's headlines had nothing to do with my competition performance.

Kiira was dripping sexiness, just look at those photos!—*Iltalehti*, January 25, 2010

License and registration! Kiira Korpi's police character gave basement-dwellers dreams of being arrested by her.—*Ilta-Sanomat*, January 25, 2010

The headlines were a shock. I never imagined these kinds of reactions to the costume and to the strip-down moment. My image in the media had always been girl-next-door, not sex bomb. I was troubled by this kind of publicity. I was worried if my family would be judged and what the sponsors and the federation would think. I had thought that the program was playful and sporty. To this day people come up to me and say they remember my police outfit. Even some police officers make jokes about it.

Maybe people weren't as judgmental as I believed. Toward the

The scandalous cop outfit, 2010. Only when other skaters started to whistle at me did I realize what kind of attention performing in a police costume would provoke (photograph by Sari Gustafsson, Lehtikuva).

end of my career, the figure skating federation asked me to perform the police routine at the Finlandia Trophy gala, but I didn't want to do that. First, I thought the program wasn't so unique in terms of choreography, and second, I didn't think it was a fitting way to say farewell to the Finnish audience in one of my last performances for them. Who knows, maybe I will dust off that program again, but it has to be in the right situation, and it has to feel right.

I think for many young skaters (like I was) it's not easy to come to terms with your body and your sexuality. In our sport the body is usually seen as a machine that produces incredible tricks on the ice. While performing you're expected to be emotionally and physically expressive in sync with the music, and your expressive moves are worked out with a confidence that doesn't necessarily match what you're feeling inside. Off the ice it's hard to know how to relate to your body and emotions other than as a tool to be kept in shape and sensations to be kept in check. Your gender and sexual expression are also things that are often not so freely explored; the tension between who you are and who you seem to be is brought to a crisis point when you're out there in public so often. At least that was the case with me. That's probably why the sexual remarks about my police costume were a shock—sex was the very last thing on my mind as I was gearing up for that show! It would be interesting to know, though, if my manager and the choreographer of the program were as surprised about these comments as I was.

As an aspiring feminist I've only recently started to think more deeply about female sports and how they are (or aren't!) represented in the media and the centrality of outward appearance, how that often seems to get more attention in the media than the actual performance. It is estimated that in the United States women make up 40 percent of all participants in sports but receive only 4 percent of sports media coverage (outside the Olympics).* I never really thought about these issues when I was competing, but the more I have begun to educate myself, the more clearly I see problems in the overly patriarchal sports structures.

My first competition outfit was purchased from a flea market when I was seven, and it was more of an outfit for gymnastics than for figure skating. It didn't have a single sequin. I wasn't at all a person who got excited about tutu-style dresses, not at home, not at the rink, although for many other girls, sparkly pink dreamy dresses were one of the best things about the sport. Once Mom asked Dad to bring me a skating outfit from a work trip in Canada. A cheapskate, Dad bought a skating outfit with so much room for growth that it's probably still too big for me today. Until I was 14, I wore hand-me-downs from older skaters, and it

---

* https://en.unesco.org/sites/default/files/gender_equality_in_sports_0.mp4.

wasn't until the junior world championship in 2003 that I wore my first competition outfit that was bought new and just for me. It was a light blue velvet dress with a chiffon hem and glittery sequins.

When I won European championship bronze in 2007, the fashion reporter Sami Sykkö suggested that his friend Tuomas Merikoski could design competition outfits for me. Sami knew figure skating because he had skated at a competitive level until he was 13. Merikoski worked in Paris for Givenchy. This was a great opportunity to work with a top designer and bring something new and different to the ice. Tuomas' outfits caused a stir as they looked nothing like the typical figure skating wardrobe. For my short program with Piazzolla's *Triunfal* music, his outfit featured a shiny black faux leather top and a short black-and-white striped skirt. I liked how modern and rebellious it was. Comments started to come in from all sides. At the national team camp in August the word was that my stripy outfit was very odd. Outfits are not figured into the score but they do influence the perception of the performance as a whole, so I was on my guard. Despite all the negative feedback, I was brave enough to stay the course, and my stripy outfit became a hit on the international scene. Slowly the talk in the locker room went from "that outfit is weird" to "oh, how cool and edgy."

In the next few seasons with Tuomas' wardrobes, I wasn't always courageous and ended up making some concessions to the judges' subjective comments. Sometimes I regretted giving in to the pressure. In my free program in the Zagreb European championships in January 2008, I skated in a silver-white outfit that attracted some disapproval. I gave in and decided to go back to a more traditional choice for the world championships in Gothenburg, Sweden, in March. The feedback was that the outfit was "lost on the white ice." I skated the same program in the world championships in a bright pink dress that was to the liking of more conventional tastes. Oh, well.

Tuomas then created an incredible light green dress with a black strap and bow on my waist. I heard that judges didn't like the "black thing interrupting my waistline." We got rid of that, making the outfit more judge friendly. I wore it throughout the rest of the season. In Vancouver I also skated in some non-traditional outfits: a long-sleeved neon yellow costume for the short program and a futuristic outfit with big shoulder pads and a zipper down the front. I had come a long way since that first flea market find. The total price of a dress in my Merikoski period easily came to two to three thousand euros depending on how

My famous black and white dress designed by Tuomas Merikoski, Euros, 2008 (Elina PAASONEN / Aamulehti).

many crystals were glued on. With new choreography and new outfits, I was spending as much as 20,000 euros more some years. It was totally worth it. My approach was to do everything I could to get to the top. Sponsor income ensured that money wasn't an obstacle to getting the best quality collaborations for every aspect of my programs.

Kiira Korpi

After the Olympic season I wanted to experiment with new choreographers and outfit designers. Your moods and styles change over time. It's fun to explore innovative and graphically striking designs. Other times you want to go for a more traditionally feminine and ornate look. That was one reason I started a collaboration with Teemu Muurimäki. Tuomas Merikoski's outfits had been inventive and gorgeous, but I wanted to go with my instinct, which was pointing to a shift in taste. Arthur introduced me to Teemu, who was working in Milano for Armani at the time. Teemu's sensibility was classical and elegant but also fresh. It wasn't merely feminine, but it had a sort of inner boldness, an assertiveness.

I really liked the way Teemu worked with me. I would send him the music for the program and share my ideas about the theme, after which Teemu worked up one or two drafts. For a clothing designer for skaters it's not just a matter of the look. Outfits had to be ice-tested to see if they could survive. The seams had to be durable and at the same time sewn in such a way that I wouldn't be distracted during a skate. Terrible to be itchy in the rink! Teemu did wonderfully and we collaborated right to the end of my career. He designed my wedding dress.

The contrast between my performing outfits and my everyday style is huge. Basically, I like to wear big floppy sweaters. With Arthur, my sense of style might have slightly expanded, but I still don't particularly like shopping. My style is very basic, and I prefer high-quality, practical fabrics. Still, I do like to dress up for a party and now even wear heels sometimes.

> Kiira was very ambitious when it came to her outfits, as they needed to speak the same language as the choreography and the music. Kiira controlled the big picture herself. I never met Kiira's coach or choreographer, but all the strings were in Kiira's hands. I feel that Kiira still let me have the designer's freedom to innovate outfits freely, and it made the work pleasant and enjoyable.—Teemu Muurimäki, designer

≥ 16 ≤

When Nothing
Is Enough

In June 2010 I had a serious discussion with my team. I wanted to set up a four-year plan with a very specific goal in mind—an Olympic medal at Sochi in 2014. I was completely convinced that only great success could give me the feeling of fulfillment I was longing for. I was ready to put everything on the line. I didn't comprehend that the fire burning inside me could not be put out with a win or a medal.

Laura Lepistö's results motivated me to train harder than ever. When Laura won world championship bronze in the summer of 2009, I wanted to believe that I could also reach the top. My plan was to snag the Olympic medal by getting steadily better every year, even every month. I calculated that my average score per competition could reach nearly 200 points, which would be enough for that medal I so badly wanted. In order to get to these numbers, I had to have a higher success rate. That meant fewer failed jumps and more perfectly executed jumps. During the Vancouver Olympic season, my free programs had only been in the 50 percent range. I decided that in two years I needed to ramp the success rate up to 90 percent. I wanted to win a European championship medal every year, and in the world championship competition, I needed to win at least one medal by 2013 at the latest to have some real momentum toward my Olympic dreams.

I had never been so explicit with my goals, but then again, I had never built my goals around specific competition results. And maybe it wasn't such a good idea. Would it work? Would it burn me out? Or would it launch me to a new level? Before the four-year plan, I had agreed with my coaches that my goals should be oriented around performing, being in the moment, not obsessing about a particular placement at a particular competition. This shift of attitude raised new questions about my motivations. Maybe I had never articulated such concrete goals because I was terrified of failure? I wanted so badly to be a winner. Maybe I needed to have a lot more belief in myself? The questions were overwhelming, but one thing I did feel confident about was that if I did my best performance on a given day, a medal would be possible in any competition.

When I first met Arthur, he would ask me about my goals. I mumbled something about my potential and how I could still develop.

"Is your goal a medal or not? Is your goal to be the best figure skater in the world or what?" Arthur insisted.

All the pieces were in place for me to push hard for a big victory at the Olympics. But I wondered if I was just making more trouble for myself with this extreme new plan. I thought, though, hadn't I been experiencing intensity and anxiety all along? I had always been very hard on myself. No matter what happened "out there," my fiercest battle was inside. It was painful to watch recordings of my programs. They reminded me of my imperfect skills, and my mistakes were out there for all to see. If I didn't skate a clean program, I would have a terrible, sinking feeling. Other times, I skated with real passion, and I yearned to show people what I could do.

The problem wasn't that I was ambitious. It's OK to be ambitious. The problem was that I thought success was a cure for everything. It was not a good sign that in the past, wins had not brought peace of mind. I was still stuck on the idea, though. Maybe it was because the success wasn't great *enough*. What if I made it to the top level? Would *that* be enough? I had to know. Being a hyper-perfectionist is maybe something that many figure skaters have in common. It's hard for us to feel 100 percent satisfaction even when we win. If I made mistakes in a program, I was shattered. Was that me or just the nature of my sport? Based on my conversations with people in many other sports, including race car driving, I think it's something we perfectionists share!

At the 2017 world championships in Helsinki, I heard Yuzuru Hanyu's acceptance speech. Instead of talking joyfully about getting to the top, he singled out a mistake in his short program and apologized for it. I wanted to shake him: "Wake up, you've just won the world championship gold!" (But why didn't I wake *myself* up too?!) I guess we perfectionism-prone skaters are always in search of the "perfect" performance, but that only happens maybe once or twice in an entire career. Yet that was my quest!

16. *When Nothing Is Enough*

I have a feeling that Kiira was very afraid of failure, but the desire for performing and success maybe was a compensation for that feeling. Then it became self-destructive, just forcing a jump on the ice again and again. In the end this will create excessive anxiety.—Anuliisa Uotila, figure skating coach and national team head coach, 2002–2012

On I went. In the years 2010 through 2012, I had the best results ever. I was the first and still the only Finnish skater to win a Grand Prix, which I did twice, in Paris in 2010 and in Moscow 2012. I made it to the European championship podium in 2011 after a four-year break, and I managed to brighten my bronze into a silver medal the following season. In the world championships I reached my personal best, ninth place, and in the Finnish championships I won first place far ahead of the field. And yet, and yet, the feeling of fulfillment eluded me.

The Europeans and worlds are a big deal, but I value Grand Prix wins highly as well. I was always reluctant to miss Grand Prix events. The International Skating Union invites only the best skaters to them. In each competition there are 12 participants, meaning that getting into the top three means beating the most talented skaters in the world. The GP competitions are also a way to get your name out there. My success was noticed in major skating countries like Japan and the United States, where European championships aren't as noticed. Additionally, there is significant prize money, which isn't too common in my sport.

Snippets from my training diary, 2010–2012:

"Next season a more relaxed attitude to life. Relax, skating is supposed to be fun."

"Fear and nervousness in the competition. My will to succeed is so bad that it hinders...."

"How much can my head take? Close to a nervous breakdown...."

My obsession with perfect performances dominated my mind in those years, which you can see in my training journal. Something was changing profoundly in the way I thought—and not in a good way. My former ability to have fun was disappearing, draining away with every competition, every round of self-criticism. Seppo's questionnaires started to bring back scarier results.

You can't completely get distance from work outside work: **Agree**

You often have feelings of inadequacy: **Agree**

You feel like you're emotionally distant from your work colleagues: **Agree**

121

When you started your current profession, you expected more achievement than you have accomplished: **Completely Agree**

I think about work related issues in my free time: **Completely Agree**

All the signs pointed to a dangerous escalation of negative thinking, but I couldn't help myself. I desperately tried to manage the pressure and especially my own expectations with visualization training and by writing down my feelings. I would go through my programs in my mind (sometimes I listened to my competition program music at the same time, other times I just played the music in my mind) focusing on specific jumps in slow motion and at normal speed. This was a great technique, but in terms of my emotional health, it had an OCD quality and amplified the stress and self-consciousness.

My training diary was full of skittish thoughts, worries, attempts at talking myself down:

> *You are the world's loveliest and best Kiira, no matter how Kiira Korpi skates. When you feel excited and nervous in competitions, it's a good sign because the body is getting ready for what's coming next. Kiira is a hard-headed performer! If a mistake happens, it's life and we move on. Trust your body to know the music and your movements will come automatically. If you sleep badly before a competition, it's OK because your body is just getting ready and you have rested enough. When you have a stomachache, you know it's just the body getting ready. If you are feeling worried or afraid, it's normal and you can leave them be as you have trained well and you know what you are doing. Remember that skating is just skating, and not the most important thing in the world. If a warm-up doesn't go great, it's fine, because only the competition performance matters. Let Maare's attitude and ambition motivate you, she brings energy and calms you down. You have a lot of tolerance and reserve. Trust your body and your little brain, which can perform well regardless of how you start. Being nervous that you have a cold or a sore leg doesn't matter because the mind is stronger and can overcome all obstacles. Be grateful that you get to perform in front of a great audience. You get strength from the competition and don't worry if the others are in top condition or not. Let Arthur cherish you and enjoy that you get to share the experience with your loved one.*

OK, but now even Arthur was starting to worry.

I can't say that being at Kiira's competitions were joyful for me per se. Kiira was really stressed out. The competition came with a lot of nervousness, expectations, and when the situation was over—win or lose—there was so much crying. I supported Kiira constantly, but that was not enough.—Arthur Borges, Kiira's husband

16. When Nothing Is Enough

My outsized drive and ambition had made me into an international level skater but was taking a big toll on me. My own expectations were already sky high, but then pile on those coming from outside, from supporters, from family, from coaches, and from the media—that increased the mental pressure even more. And, ironically, each success brought even more self-doubt.

In April 2011 I traveled to the world championships in Moscow. The competition had been moved to Russia after Japan had been hit with a tsunami and was held a month later than planned. A few months prior I had medaled at the European championship, and with the extra prep, I was in top shape.

Training with her before Moscow, I was sure that Kiira would win the world championships. I remember clearly one moment at the Hakametsä training arena with Susanna. We were rinkside where the Zamboni drives in. Kiira was practicing her program and we had tears running down our cheeks. I was thinking that there couldn't be another skater as good as her. I was sure that Kiira would beat everyone straight up.—Maaret Siromaa, Kiira's coach, 1996–2013

The situation before the 2011 world championships in Moscow was exceptional in my career, as I often went to a competition feeling my programs still needed a lot of work, or I would have the flu or tummy ache, or I was injured. Not this time! After that winter and spring I was in such good shape that I rarely missed a jump in practice. But even though I was in the best shape of my life, I beat myself up for the minor mistakes I made in training. A few weeks before the world championships, I was going through my free program, just fine tuning, keeping it fresh. It was almost flawless, but then a planned triple jump turned into a double jump. Usually no big deal, especially as I'd been skating really, really well. This devastated me. After practice I locked myself in the bathroom of the arena to cry and cry and cry. I still remember some of the self-critical and unrealistic questions I asked myself. How could I succeed in the world championships if I couldn't achieve absolutely clean performances in practice? Later on I realized how self-destructive my thoughts were. Why wasn't I content with my obvious progress? Why did I have to nitpick even the most positive practices? By not giving myself credit, I was sabotaging myself.

I was sometimes quite worried about Kiira, especially when she seemed to be crying all the time. This wasn't typical for Kiira at all, and it was a sign that things were not OK. Still those situations and reasons behind all the crying were never really discussed, because from week to week there was always some competition or special event coming up. It was living in that sportsworld bubble.—Petra Korpi, older sister

In Moscow everything continued to go well in training. Jumping felt effortless and easy, the timing was there. Then came the competition. I remember my legs going numb right at the start of my short program. I fell in my first jump combination. I was shocked. How could I have missed this combination when I did it so perfectly and consistently in training?! As I finished up the short, I was angry and determined that I would do a clean free program. Next day, free program. Come on, Kiira, you can do it.

I didn't skate badly but certainly not as good as in practice, and by the end, I was left far from the top, ninth place. Still, it was the best world championship showing of my career, but it was a huge disappointment compared to the expectations going in. I had made skating too big of a thing in my mind, and it was my mind that betrayed me. Looking back to it now, I feel that I was even more afraid of big success than big failure.

One and a half years later I returned to the same arena in Moscow. That's where I won my second GP competition

Moscow Grand Prix win, 2012 (Elina Paasonen / Aamulehti).

and qualified for the world GP final. I made Finnish skating history as the first skater from my country to accomplish that. But sadly, I had worked myself up into such a state that I was incapable of fully appreciating it.

There I was with my friends and family at that dinner at the Café Pushkin. I was supposed to be celebrating, but I was utterly distracted by my racing thoughts. My mind went back to the fall in the loop, the mistake in the short program and the personal best score that I thought still too low. Of course, this wasn't the first time I suffered from perfectionistic thinking, but what was different now was my awareness.

Everyone seemed happy and I probably seemed happy to everyone, too, but I certainly didn't *feel* happy. And because I had just achieved one of the biggest wins of my skating career, these thoughts and feelings were more distressing than ever. An icky feeling of shame washed over me, and I kept thinking: "What is so deeply wrong with me that I can never be satisfied?"

> As a support group we were very close to Kiira, but we still didn't get how badly she was truly feeling.—Mikko Luukkaa, manager

☞ 17 ☜

Text Message

By the spring of 2013 my trust in Susanna and Maare had broken down. It looked like the end was coming for us. How did things get to this point? Let's step back a few months.

The fall of 2012 was brutal on my body. I did both the China and the Moscow Grand Prix competitions in the space of only two weeks. I performed well, and my overall score was enough to qualify for the Grand Prix final in December back in Russia, in Sochi. My team started to plan the trip. But now my back was so sore that I could barely practice. I focused mainly on visualization training. Then, two weeks before Sochi, I was hit with norovirus, and my strength drained away even more. Of course, my problems were all over the media. This put me in a familiar position, fighting back from a tough spot. Would this give me the grit to finish strongly or bring me down? Maare, Susanna, Seppo and I figured that there were two options: I either opt out of the competition and take care of my health, or I go to Sochi and try my best no matter how ill or unprepared I felt. Guess which option I chose?

I took the trip. Flash forward. I'm in the rink and the music is starting up. I immediately start moving, pure survival mode. My only thought is to get through it any way I can. Almost completely exhausted, I skate my short and my free the next day. I place fourth out of six skaters.

I should have been happy—the first Finnish skater to ever make it to the Grand Prix final and then to place fourth! But there was no time to celebrate or take a breather. Five days after the GP final were the Finnish championships in Joensuu. I knew that expectations were through the roof. I also knew that I was mentally and physically drained. I wanted to skip it, but the Finnish championship is a major deal for the local club in Joensuu and for the Finnish skating federation, which informed me I was required to skate unless there was a compelling medical reason not to. My left Achilles tendon had started to act up after the GP final. I didn't realize how terrible it was going to get, not yet. Mikko empathized with me and had a heated conversation with Maare and Susanna, who didn't want to see me pull out. In the end, I skated in Joensuu and won Finnish championship gold. The scoring gap between me and the silver medalist Juulia Turkkila was almost 35 points, even though I skated my worst free program of the season. I limped away from that win in a world of pain and too exhausted to take in the victory once again.

I then took my Christmas break—just four days. The pain in my Achilles tendon did not go away. It got much worse. The tendon was clearly inflamed and swollen. I couldn't practice at all. It hurt just to walk. I was so sad that I needed to skip the European championships in January, and I had had such a successful fall season! I put my full focus on recovery so I might be OK by the 2013 world championships in Canada in March. I started doing some jumps in practice at the beginning of February and we hoped I would be back at a high level of fitness by the end of that month. But the pain came roaring back and I had to skip the world championships, too. I had not been able to take part in the world championships the year before either, due to hamstring and hip injuries. The cycle of injuries seemed to be accelerating.

Every day I woke up anxious, impatient, and worried. I didn't get to practice in a steady and organized way for about five months, which is an eternity in figure skating. At the same time, I feared the top skaters in the world were improving fast and that I would not be able to catch up to them. I got lots of hard stares from my team. Susanna was especially frustrated, as she had big plans for me. I felt my coaches had been disappointed with me for a long time. What made it worse was that nothing was ever said out loud.

I guess that it wasn't always easy for Maare and Susanna to coach me, even if I was usually super motivated and goal oriented. On the other hand, if I wasn't feeling well, everyone knew it. And I was easily thrown off my game. If I had an assignment due at school, if I tweaked a muscle or tendon, or if there was a TV interview coming up—any of these things could affect my practice sessions. Susanna and Maare felt helpless in these situations.

Susanna was more easily disappointed because she had a pre-established idea of what I needed to do next. But she also didn't make room for *my* ideas. We were often in a silent battle. Susanna got easily upset if *her* plans didn't work out and I got disheartened if *my* plans didn't work out. Meanwhile, Maare's natural generosity and sense of play was cramped. I remember being a little girl training with Maare and feeling that I could skate forever. But now there was no safe space for any of us to be fully ourselves. Over time, the three of us had pushed aside uncomfortable feelings and thoughts, and lots of things that needed to be said weren't. I can see how this might work in a crunch time, in the short-term, but in the long run, the tension builds up and becomes something darker.

I admit I was unpredictable. My coaches didn't know which Kiira would show up at practice—I might be depressed and pouty or ready to sail across the ice with a giant smile on my face. But I wasn't the only moody one. I also walked on eggshells, wondering what mood the coach would be in on any given day, especially Susanna, who seemed to be more on edge. This was a common worry among skaters. Would the coach walk in and start yelling at us for some minor mistake or would we be encouraged and uplifted? I guess we all carry seeds of fear and love inside of us, and whichever seed we choose to nourish the most will grow the most.

> At times we had a rough time with Kiira—especially in situations when I came to practice with a detailed plan. But then Kiira would show up with no energy to do anything, maybe because things were going badly for her. In those moments I should have had more understanding, but I wasn't always able to. We felt disappointment on both sides.—Susanna Haarala, Kiira's coach, 2002–2013

Being a good coach means sensing when an athlete needs to be pushed and when understanding, gentle care and total acceptance is called for. I think a coach doesn't need to listen to every last complaint and pay attention to feelings all the time. Still, as a young athlete, I needed much more understanding than I was getting. I also needed to express the full range of emotions, to have permission to just be human.

As we got into that crazy 2012 season of back-to-back events, I felt like nothing that I did satisfied them anymore. Sometimes I felt that they were ganging up on me, and when Seppo joined our meetings, he was always on their side—three against one. They were the experts; they knew best. This was so different from today's athlete-centered approach in coaching. I think the coach's primary role should be to provide the space for the athlete to grow and to build their own inner wisdom, not to impose their own style on the athlete.

My coaches thought I was being childish when I was "feeling too much" or "thinking too much," and it was just a matter of toughing out the training, toughing it out mentally and physically. At the time, I actually believed this; I believed being sensitive was my weakness. When I switched coaches later, the same pattern repeated itself. Thank God I now know that my sensitivity—my ability to think, feel, listen and perceive *deeply*—is my number one strength in sports and in life. Likewise, emotional intelligence and communication skills are the greatest assets for any coach or teacher, too.

As a team, Maare and Susanna and I did try to address the problems in the relationship, and I'm proud of us for at least making the effort. We acknowledged that something was off, but in the end, that wasn't enough—because we were never fully up front with each other. Our end-of-season talks were supposed to be an opportunity to reassess, to build a better team. Instead, these sessions were dominated by fault-finding and by passive-aggressive behavior. I think all three of us were harboring some bad feelings, and unfortunately, we didn't have the emotional skills to relate to each other in a wise and sustainable way.

> When it came to coaching, Susanna and I saw eye to eye on many things, and we both agreed on where to draw the line for Kiira. I probably should have pampered Kiira more but I'm not sure it would have changed anything. Would the end result have been so different?—Maaret Siromaa, Kiira's coach, 1996–2013

One day in April 2013, I woke up with pain in my ankle again. I made the decision on my own to go to physical therapy instead of practice. I notified Susanna in a text that I wasn't coming to train that day as the range of motion in my ankle wasn't normal. I waited for her to reply. I heard a notification on my phone. A text message. I have deleted that message from my phone, and I don't remember it word for word, but what it said is burned in my mind. The softer version without the curse words went something like this: "Our star has a locked-up ankle again, and she is not coming to ice. Why don't we ever learn that we shouldn't waste our time with this?"

The message was meant for Maare but had been sent to me by accident. I was deeply offended. How could my own coaches speak about me like that? And was Maare on board with this kind of talk? Our boat was sinking fast, and the text message only made it worse, much worse. I called Susanna and confronted her. She said she was sorry for not being able to share her feelings with me openly. If I remember correctly, she wasn't sorry about the message per se, but sorry that she wasn't able to speak her mind earlier. She burst into tears. Susanna said that she and Maare had been feeling helpless for a long time and that nothing they did seemed to help me. I knew that it could not have been easy to train me. My moods and the string of injuries must have been extremely frustrating to my coaches, but still, it was so sad that the truth had to come out in this way. Now that I wasn't healthy and able to bring them success anymore, I was "a waste of time" for them.

On the other hand, the text message was a blessing and a relief. At least now I knew how they (or at least Susanna) truly felt about coaching me by then. It was now obvious that I had been at a dead end in my training with them for a while. In particular, the off-ice training Susanna wanted me to do did not fit my own intuition about what was right for me. I believed (and still believe) that the body should be strengthened from the inside out rather than the outside in. What does that mean? It means that no matter the age of the skater, everything we do should be with an inner understanding, an intention, so that even when we're hitting the gym to do squats or sit-ups, we're fully on board with the program. How can coaches and athletes get to this place? I think the coach has to encourage the young athlete to express their feelings and beliefs so that they can develop a strong sense of self-ownership and direction of their *own* sports careers. It all starts with the ability of the individual person to be sensitive to what's going on in their own mind and body. This is the foundation of a strong athletic practice. It requires a lot of inner work and self-reflection on the coach's part, which is a type of education that I'd love to see included more in coaching programs.

When I did Susanna's various strengthening routines, such as lunges and weightlifting, I started to feel that there was not much of a connection to my on-ice performance. It was like *someone else* was there in the gym doing those routines. Many of Susanna's exercises were probably very good in and of themselves, but they did not fit into my overall growth and the reality of my performance style. I can still recall moments of sheer pointlessness in the gym at the Hakametsä Arena doing lunge after lunge. I tried to explain to Susanna that my body felt twisted and that the lunges weren't organic to me.

"You are thinking way too much, Kiira. You just need to do it. It will come together," Susanna would say.

Susanna did try to search for variations to the off-ice routines and consulted various experts, but her overall approach didn't change radically. I thought that I wasn't benefitting at all from the kind of weight training Susanna wanted me to do—not when I clearly felt that my technique wasn't clean and my back hurt while doing some of the moves. Susanna was still sticking to her training philosophy while I was leaning more toward the practices Jarmo (Jami) Ahonen introduced to me, where muscle balance, control and whole-body elasticity is prioritized. I trusted him because he was the one who saved me when my legs (and belly) had frozen up in 2009. Jami often spoke about how the body should react like a rubber ball and bounce in every direction. I hadn't yet achieved that elasticity, and I believe that was the reason my injuries started to pile up in addition to insufficient nutrition.

Nowadays, figure skating training is moving towards a dance ethic. Male skaters today, for example, are slimmer, more agile and more flexible athletes than the more muscular skaters of the early 2000s. Jami's personality as a trainer was also the opposite of what I had become used to. He had a playful, lovely, and positive attitude toward practicing. Perhaps because he was an outsider to the sport, he didn't take himself too seriously. But it was this kind of ease and relaxed attitude that I so badly needed at that point in my career. The obsession with results and with being the "Kiira" everyone expected me to be was wearing me down. I think that for many figure skating trainers and parents, the success of their skaters is unconsciously linked to their own identity, ambition and feeling of fulfillment. Naturally, Jami also hoped that I would succeed in competitions, but ultimately, it wasn't his primary motivation. This was liberating.

> It was Kiira's job to state her decisions out loud and my job to support her in those decisions. We had been talking with Petra about changing coaches long before Kiira reached her moment, but we had to wait for Kiira to feel when the time was right. Maybe in this sport we have to look beyond Finland when we want athletes to take that next step. That was something Kiira needed to articulate herself. I supported Kiira in her decision to leave her coaches.—Mikko Luukkaa, manager

My decision to leave Maare and Susanna ripened slowly, and by the end, there were many things that just weren't working for me anymore. The text message was the last straw that encouraged me to make some big decisions. I wanted to find a coaching relationship where I didn't need to be careful of what I said but I could openly talk about my feelings. I wanted coaches who were fully behind my strategies and goals. I still wanted to get on the Olympic podium in Sochi. And I needed to train somewhere besides my hometown of Tampere.

Kiira Korpi

I chose the day and time to let everyone know I had an announcement. Maare was on sick leave then, so I called her, and then I met with Susanna and my new mental coach Satu in person. I had let Seppo go earlier that spring. It was a very painful day, and we all shed tears. I had been coached by Maare since I was eight years old, and I had spent more than ten years with Susanna. The coaches understood my decision and even seemed to welcome the change, which was a kind gesture from them. Still, I'm sure saying certain things out loud did hurt, especially when I said I had lost trust in them.

Susanna and Maare knew that they had given all they could. However, I was unable to stay healthy under their coaching, I couldn't fully trust them anymore, and I wasn't motivated to keep training by myself in the local rinks either. In fact, compared to other skaters on the international scene, I had stuck to my home turf for a long, long time. The Swiss skater Sarah Meier said she regretted two things after winning European championship gold in 2011, the last competition of her career: the fact that she didn't fully appreciate her earlier medals more and that she had never left Switzerland to experience training abroad. I didn't want to have those same regrets.

> The end of the coaching felt horrible for me and I personally took it very hard. Kiira and I had worked together for so long and had such history. Coaching Kiira influenced my life in so many ways, and it was so much more than just my job.—Maaret Siromaa, Kiira's coach, 1996–2013

> That's when I started getting worried about Kiira. Setting such a tough goal in a situation when training was practically non-existent was saying to me her mental balance was not in the best possible state.—Susanna Haarala, Kiira's coach, 2002–2013

Maare and Susanna are still dear to me and I'm grateful for all the effort they put into coaching me all those years. They were like my second mothers. I respect them as people and coaches immensely, although my own coaching philosophy is becoming very different from the way I was coached. Or maybe it is becoming similar to Maare's playful and liberating coaching philosophy that she used to have especially when I was much younger, before we all got too invested and serious. I admire how devoted they both were to their coaching work. I also very much appreciate Susanna's persistent attitude, and Maare's natural grace and open heartedness. I won't forget that under their guidance. I grew to be a championship medalist. But I must ask: how much further and deeper could we have reached had our minds, souls and bodies been more connected and free?

> The role of figure skating coaching is to be utterly devoted, which might create anxiety at times. If a coach is on your back all the time, the athlete won't succeed. One characteristic of a successful athlete is the ability to know when to be truly autonomous, as no one in the world can help you in the middle of a performance. Kiira was such a strong soul and wonderful athlete that I doubt she would have let anyone else make the final adjustments for her when she stepped on the ice.—Anuliisa Uotila, figure skating coach and national team head coach, 2002–2012

Moments I Wish Could Go On Forever

There's only this moment, the notes starting to wash over me, the movement just about to start, my eyes focusing far, far off. The music sparks and starts me moving. As the speed picks up, I lose myself. My coaches warned me—stay grounded in the program. Maare knew I was a dreamer. I have to hold on to that focus on the technicals. I have to.

But then the pull of the music. I trust the music as it brings out emotion after emotion. The melodies wash over me and call me into another realm. Ah! How much I love to skate and be with the rhythm, the audience and that wide, wide space. I wish it could always be like this. I feel the energy move through me to the tips of my fingers, like electricity. All the years of work are coming together when you're in flow, when step follows step, jump follows jump. Before I know it, it's over.

Now, final position. I wish I could stay here forever. I'm breathless, still full to the brim with music. This feels so right.

⇒ 18 ⇐

A New Beginning

I had heard good things about Rafael Arutyunyan for years. The first time I met him was in California in the mid-aughts when I attended a camp at the same training center where he had coached my idol Michelle Kwan. Rafael had been born in the former Soviet Union, in Georgia, and had moved to the United States to establish a coaching practice. Besides Kwan, he had coached many other top skaters in the world including Mao Asada, Sasha Cohen, and Jeffrey Buttle, all of whom were world championship multi-medalists. I knew that Rafael was a very skilled coach, especially for jump technique, which was the area that I needed to strengthen. There was a special urgency for me because around the world, jump technique was ramping up quite a bit. Just a few competition seasons before I moved to California, a triple toe loop-triple toe loop combination was considered state of the art for female skaters, but now the difficulty level had taken a huge leap forward, with teenage Russian skaters leading the way. I contacted Rafael to ask if he would train me that summer in California. Rafael answered in his strong Russian accent that he only agreed to coach committed and hardworking athletes. I had found my new coach.

Somehow, rumors about my upcoming coaching switch had already begun swirling in Finland. With all the talk going on, we asked the figure skating federation to make the formal announcement that I was moving from Tampere to the United States to train with Rafael. Naturally, I didn't speak publicly about the discussions I had with Maare and Susanna but only said that I needed a "radical change" in order to progress in my career. It was true that my coaching options were limited. I couldn't stay in Finland, I didn't want to go to Russia, and the other figure skating centers in Europe, in Milan and Oberstdorf, didn't feel right at the time. I wanted to work in an environment where I would be surrounded by strong skaters. The move to California also felt good because I had good memories of camp there.

18. A New Beginning

I was almost 23 and at the time one of the oldest skaters on the international scene. I missed the feeling of being with people my age. Rafael's coaching team included, for example, former U.S. champion Ashley Wagner, who was three years younger than me and whose technique had been dramatically enhanced under Rafael's guidance. When we were training and competing together, we were not very close, but recently, after she retired, we've had some really interesting conversations.

In Finland we have club-based coaching. It's not a culture where you have "a star coach" paired with "star skaters." Maare and Susanna were Tappara coaches, not my personal coaches. Another unique thing about the Finnish club system: My coaches received the same salary whether I was in the club or not. Even when my career took off, they continued to coach skaters of all age groups, dozens of skaters daily. In public, Maare and Susanna were very consistent about not giving the impression that they were only "Kiira Korpi's coaches." I believe that coaching me was mostly rewarding for them, and I also appreciated that it required a lot more time and work than the coaching they did for other Tappara skaters.

In many other countries, coaching has developed around famous coaches, not clubs. Coaches can choose the athlete they want to work with, and star coaches mainly only choose championship-level skaters or great future prospects. The pay structure is also different, with coaches being hired for one-on-one time in the rink. The coaches are selling their know-how like bread at a bakery, and it's up to the skaters and their families to find the funds to hire them. In California, I usually bought one or two 20-minute daily sessions from Rafael, since he wouldn't have had the time for more.

We trained that summer in Lake Arrowhead, a sweet mountain town, a one-and-a-half-hour drive from Los Angeles. Then, the arena closed, and we moved our training operation inland, to the town of Artesia. I lived near the ocean on Hermosa Beach and left for the ice rink early in the morning. As I rode along the coast, I would pass groups of people going surfing. It was so lovely to be living that close to the ocean, but it was also a shame that I couldn't enjoy life as much as my neighbors who headed out to the beach or had backyard barbecues. I had traveled all over the world during my career, including to the United States, but the move to California was still a culture shock for me. People I didn't know called me "honey," "dear," and "sweetheart" and asked how I was doing all the time. How am I doing? Got to think about that!

But living in America was great because it allowed me to grow as a person. I started to feel like I was in a place where no one had any preconceptions about me. It was liberating. At the same time, I was lonely and anxious, even more than in Finland, where I could always see my family and friends. There were times when I felt envious of foreign skaters. I sometimes thought I should have gone abroad sooner and I would have been a better skater. Now I realize this hunger to constantly outperform would have probably swallowed me up earlier than it did. What I needed as a young skater wasn't to always be trying to be the best but to have a life that was more in balance.

Because of the Achilles injury I had sustained some months earlier, I was unable to practice with Rafael as much as I wanted, but I kept learning throughout that season. I soon noticed that he was extraordinarily skilled at building jumping technique and had a very strong character. Once you understand the basic principles and the physics of throwing your spinning body into the air, the whole technique becomes more efficient and looks infinitely more natural. The proof is in the pudding: Nathan Chen developed under Rafael's tutelage to be the first skater to complete five quad jumps in a competition. I respect Rafael as a technical coach greatly, but the psychological and emotional approach he took to his coaching didn't appeal to me at all.

As an experienced athlete and a person interested in psychology, I wasn't impressed by Rafael's yelling, insulting, and teasing. Unfortunately, this type of behavior is not uncommon in competitive rinks in the United States and around the world. At the rink in California, I was shocked to see skaters crying on the ice on a daily basis, while coaches (and parents) were screaming at them or emotionally neglecting them. What makes me sad is that most of the people at the rink—skaters, parents, coaches, officials—most of them become socialized into that culture of intimidation. Thank God more and more people, myself included, are starting to wake up from the insane illusion that it is somehow "normal" or even good for the athlete to be emotionally, psychologically and sometimes physically punished. Rafael often called skaters cowards if a jump attempt turned into a popped jump— "You're such a chicken!"

And this was his tamest comment.

I was spared from his more outrageous words, but I frequently saw him yell at other skaters, sometimes very young ones. There were even times when Rafael called Ashley names and had big showdowns with her. I don't know where figure skating coaches get their colorful animal-themed insults. I seem to recall Russian coaching legend Alexei Mishin calling one of his skaters a little Russian worm. Is this an insult or an endearment? Or a sign of a really twisted power imbalance? Cow and pig are very common insults in the skating circles, too. For some skaters this type of coaching seems to work, and they perform better when they are angry or scared—at least for a while, or with dramatic consequences for their long-term health.

Rafael's training team was powered by his wife Vera and by Nadia Kanaeva. Vera concentrated on off-ice training, which she adapted from ballet exercises. Nadia is a former skater from Russia who got to the top of the world at the junior level, but a back injury put a halt to her career. She was a skilled skater, so smooth that she resembled an ice dancer. Just observing her had a great influence on my own style. Nadia was very precise about the smallest details. For example, she taught me to feel for the center of gravity of my foot inside the skate. She helped me to become acutely aware of when the weight needed to be more on the heel or more on the toes and how the foot itself moved. I had never thought about what my foot was doing inside the skate. In my early training I was taught to think of the foot and the skate as one unit: outside edge, inside edge and that's it.

Nadia's work was an excellent complement to Rafael's more jumping-oriented coaching, but she too could have coached with more psychological and emotional wisdom—with more inspiration and positive reinforcement. I knew she had those skills in her because sometimes when I worked on a program with her, just the two of us, it was very uplifting and joyful! But typically in regular training sessions she would hit her fist on the boards and just yell, "Push, push, push!" I remember sometimes wondering to myself whether there could be any other tip she could offer me to get more speed than to *push*.

Despite all my shortcomings, in many ways I was a model coachee. I was always on time, conscientious, and precise. I listened to directions carefully and I didn't need to be given instructions twice. I did try very hard to implement the principles and techniques I was learning. Rafael noticed it in his trademark way: "You're smart; you have a brain."

Alexei Mishin also noticed I was a thinker. I was very intense about the learning process. I never tried to be particularly intense (tried the opposite, actually), but that's just how my mind works. I adopted new techniques quickly and could almost outdo the coaches with my analysis of the new approaches. Maybe a little less analyzing might have been better for me, but then again, I think it's an absolutely wonderful quality in a person to want to be able to think for themselves and to ask the crucial question "why." Why are we training this today? Why do you think I should try the jump like you suggested? Why this, why that, why not like this? I know this type of athlete can be so irritating for a coach, but in order to get people fully engaged in the coaching process, you absolutely must be willing to answer the crucial why questions. You (the coach) might actually be surprised how much you'll learn from those questions and answers yourself, too.

> I have never met anyone with such intense and numerous thoughts. It often correlates with intelligence and Kiira is super intelligent. She has the ability to analyze things into atoms and then a lot of data is produced.—Satu Lähteenkorva, psychologist, Kiira's mental coach, 2012–2015

The relationship between coach and athlete in figure skating is intense and can become problematic, like any close relationship. Normally, the athletes are very young, in many ways immature, and in many countries, coaches are God-like authority figures. Discussions are rather one-sided. The culture of the sport reinforces the authority of the coach—after each practice session, the skater is supposed to bow and thank the coach. It reminds me of the protocols of ballet, but it's hard to imagine bowing to your coach in track and field, ice hockey, or, come to think of it, any other sport. Maybe in martial arts? Anyway, changing coaches is also perhaps more rare in figure skating than in many other sports. In team sports a youngster might have different coaches almost every season, but in figure skating it's not totally uncommon for the athlete to have the same coach throughout their whole career. Figure skaters are loyal and rarely question their coach. I, too, didn't think about changing coaches before the situation had become so dramatically dysfunctional.

To create truly healthy and flourishing coach-athlete partnerships I believe that coaches need to have excellent social, emotional and psychological skills. The coach must first do a lot of inner work and learn how to coach themselves in a positive way in order to become a steady, safe and supportive presence in their athletes' lives. I'm hopeful that the younger generation of coaches is on a mission to build the sport strong from the inside out and to train their athletes in a way that allows them to grow self-confident and balanced both mentally and physically.

> I have the feeling that if Kiira hadn't taken the step to go abroad, she wouldn't have felt that she tested her limits. I'm happy about that—although the experience was tough for Kiira, it was necessary.—Susanna Haarala, Kiira's coach, 2002–2013

≋ 19 ≋

Torn

Throughout my career I battled massive problems with health, both physical and psychological, but not until 2013 did I have an injury that required serious surgery. When I was younger, I was pretty arrogant about what my body could do. I remember being 18 years old and wondering how *anybody* could ever get injured just skating! As my competitive schedule got increasingly intense and demanding (and I started doing those crazy strict diets), it was difficult to adjust to the lifestyle, but I remained oblivious to the tremendous strain on my body and mind.

When I was 14, I had a very public and dramatic injury that looked much worse than it was. That was in 2003, in Flims, Switzerland. There were probably 35 skaters on the ice. I was in the middle of a step sequence, and of all the people to crash into, I crashed Niina Laksola, a good friend from my local club. A deep gash appeared on my shin. Blood gushed from the six-inch cut and onto the ice.

Niina started to yell, Henna Hietala pressed the edges of the cut together and Ari-Pekka Nurmenkari joked that now Kiira would never be Miss Finland. The ambulance took almost half an hour to get up to the mountain village. Luckily, the cut hadn't reached the artery and was stitched up in the hospital without complications. I was sent to the airport alone. I boarded the plane in a wheelchair. The airline had neglected to put my name on the passenger list, so back at the airport in Finland, my mom and dad thought for sure I'd been kidnapped and my organs were being sold on the black market. The accident left an impressive scar on my leg, but I missed only a month of practice. Not too bad.

A more serious health issue appeared in the fall of 2008. I was 20 years old and was diagnosed with esophagitis, the beginning of a series of stomach issues. These continued off and on for my whole career. When I think why my body started to break down, I see a clear connection to the continual stress, the immense pressure I put on my musculoskeletal system, not mention the restrictive eating and considerable weight loss combined with psychological issues such as paralyzing fear of gaining weight. That year, I missed eight months of competition appearances and couldn't practice for three of those months.

The longer my career went on, the more injuries I accumulated: spinal disc, ankle, hip, back, Achilles tendon, shoulder, and exercise-induced asthma. The house of cards started to come down. One injury immediately followed the other. I think that the natural coordination between my muscles gradually fell apart due to unrelenting practice but also due to the emotional trauma I constantly sustained. It was as if my body was breaking down piece by piece in proportion to how my mind and soul were shattering apart. Of course, at the time I wasn't able to make this connection. I won a major competition medal in the European championships in Sheffield in January 2012, but after that I had to skip the next seven major championships, seven competitions when I was supposed to be at my peak. No wonder my team and I were running out of patience.

> When Kiira had those ailments, it didn't help that she was surrounded by so many different opinions and treatment methods. I felt that the healthcare team was at one time so big that I wondered how well information was communicated and coordinated. Who was really responsible for her treatment?—Susanna Haarala, Kiira's coach, 2002–2013

> Kiira kind of needed permission to train. Unless the doctor reassured Kiira that she could practice again, she didn't really dare to start training. She was afraid she would break something else. This was sometimes difficult for us as we didn't always have time to wait it out.—Maaret Siromaa, Kiira's coach, 1996–2013

In an interesting but not very surprising way, the long injury breaks were a huge psychological relief for me, especially toward the end of my career. I was of course very sad and disappointed that I needed to throw in the towel again and again. The truth is, though, that without these enforced breaks, I would have probably collapsed mentally and emotionally even earlier than I did. The injuries gave me a breather from the intense routine, my compulsive goals, and toxic training environments. The injuries were my body and mind's way of throwing me down and telling me, "That's enough now, Kiira—you have to take care of yourself!"

During these breaks I had time to explore those issues that contributed to the injuries in the first place. I always tried to make the most of these challenging periods. In fact, after every recovery period, I came back a better skater than I had been before the injury. Why? Because my mental and physical work were more organic and more wholesome. The top-down control by my coaches was absent for a while, and I felt liberated and free to be guided by my own intuition and inner wisdom. I studied the nuances in the choreography that had been designed so wonderfully for me, and when I was able to eventually get back to the physical work, I focused on the fundamentals. Training the fundamentals with a proper technique made so much sense to me and I whole-heartedly enjoyed it. Unfortunately, many times skaters, even very young children, are pushed to train on the difficult elements too early, which can lead to injuries and distract them from the pure joy of learning new things.

The layoffs made me a more well-rounded skater. In the last few years of my career I scored well across all the point categories, which are a combination of technical and artistic elements. The exercises I did by myself in rehabilitation training, such as water running, felt often more satisfying and more strengthening than my practice routine during a normal season. When I did high-stakes triple jumps under the judgmental and nervous eye of a top coach, I didn't sense as much progress. And most of all, I didn't sense as much freedom to be me—imperfect. On the ice I often felt like I was wearing an emotional straitjacket. After rehab periods, though, my attitude shifted—for a while. When I returned to the rink after weeks or months of not being able to skate, I had a rush of happiness and confidence. Unfortunately, the feeling of grace and gratefulness soon trailed away when the old familiar strict coaching patterns returned, and I lost the connection to my own inner compass.

> Whether her injuries were big or small, Kiira always came back with even better skills after a recovery period. The changes might include more physical strength, better posture, more control. When skills have to be relearned there is room for freedom and a chance for things to be done differently. You can give up your own manners. The quality of Kiira's skills improved.—Susanna Haarala, Kiira's coach, 2002–2013

> I didn't see Kiira's mental tiredness. I was just wondering how on Earth can this person always gather the will to condition herself after those injuries. I think Kiira's tiredness was due to the continuous new injuries. The psyche was stronger than the body.—Brita Korpi, mother

19. Torn

Mikko's plane landed in Los Angeles in September 2013. Finland was 9000 kilometers behind him, far from the lovely weather in California that day, sun breaking through clouds and about 75 degrees Fahrenheit. I had lived and trained in the United States for about three months by then. Mikko had drafted a detailed schedule and plan for his visit. He had come to set up photo shoots and other events to keep my sponsors happy. I was fortunate that all the bigger sponsors wanted to continue working with me, even though I had relocated to the United States. So the move to Los Angeles turned out well financially, and now there was other great news as well. Marko Yrjövuori had replied to Mikko's messages and was ready to work with me!

Marko Yrjövuori had emigrated from Finland in the '90s and become part of the massage and conditioning training team for the Los Angeles Lakers. He said his marquis job was to keep Kobe Bryant in super shape game after game. In California, Marko started helping me with the inflamed Achilles, but he soon realized that this problem was a symptom of deeper systemic issues and imbalances in the body. So we concentrated on overall conditioning and strengthening a number of key things, such as stabilizing my hips.

The doctors had prescribed anti-inflammatory drugs and said I could train as long as I didn't feel too much pain. I worked on and on with a sense of cautious optimism. However, when I returned to the ice to practice with Rafael, it was never long before the pain would return, usually within a day or two. One day the foot was fine and the next it was throbbing with agonizing pain.

It finally happened on Tuesday, September 10, 2013. I was doing some specially designed exercises to warm up the Achilles tendon and then changed into my skates, custom-made in Italy. These were sewn to perfection so the back of the skate wouldn't dig into my Achilles. I coasted onto the ice with confidence, ready to do my warm-up sequence like a thousand times before: ten minutes of loose, slow skating, then some basic steps and twizzles, and then setting my posture for jumps. Then came the first take off into an axel. One push. Just one push and—snap! I could feel my Achilles just give. A single axel isn't a jump that requires a powerful take off, but the tendon couldn't take any more and that was that.

The pain was dreadful. I was rushed to the hospital for treatment. The left Achilles tendon was 70 percent torn. I was horrified but at the same time strangely relieved. Now at least there was no more guessing, no more wondering whether to go out and train on a particular day. All the uncertainty ended with that one snap. A few days later I flew home for extended treatment. But first, I had to do a set of sponsorship shoots that Mikko had set up. I went on camera for Audi, Finnair, and Valio—on crutches and in lots of pain.

I had inquired about getting treatment in the United States, but our Olympic team doctor Harri Hakkarainen recommended returning

In Los Angeles after Achilles tendon rupture, 2013.

to Finland. There a team could keep a constant eye on my recovery. I had another set of MRIs. With the 30 percent of healthy tendon left, according to Dr. Hakkarainen, recovery would be faster without surgery. We got this diagnosis three days before the last Olympic qualifier. Maybe we all had the desperate hope that I could recover in time for Sochi. There was still actually a chance to send at least one Finn to the Olympics even if it wasn't me. That dream was definitely and permanently crushed a few days later when Juulia Turkkila tried out in the qualifiers with very short notice. She didn't earn a spot for Finland in the Sochi Olympics.

> Kiira had insurance, which covered her doctors' costs and loss of income from the start of the rehabilitation period to when the doctors said she could skate again. We were glad we had invested in high quality insurance, because it paid for top-class rehab and access to very good specialists. This level of insurance was quite rare for Finnish athletes. The prevalent thinking is that these are people in top shape, but that's not smart thinking.—Mikko Luukkaa, manager

My rehabilitation program was coordinated by physiotherapist Tuomas Sallinen, who was working with the Finnish national volleyball team at the time. Tuomas had a lot of experience and he seemed pleasant and professional. I started to execute his plan with my usual discipline. I did water aerobics and water running in the Mäkelänrinne pool, did leg work with thick elastic bands, and trained at the gym to my utmost limits. That's how I did things.

This was also a time when I was feeling more and more distant from Arthur, especially after having spent the summer in the United States. But fate sorted things out for us. Around the time of my injury, Arthur lost his job and came to Finland to live with me. For the first time in our relationship we got to live in the same country for a few months. I realized how special our relationship was. It was so comforting and beautiful to have a "normal" life with him, together every day, supporting each other through all kinds of challenges. But there was always that Achilles tendon—it just wasn't healing.

By December 2013, three months into rehab, the leg was still hurting a lot. According to the prognoses by Hakkarainen and others, I should have been at the next stage of activity by then, but after even a couple of jogging steps, I had shooting pain in my leg. I started to have some scary doubts. Maybe the pain was all in my head? I had heard that this could happen if someone has a long-lasting condition. I demanded *another* set of MRIs. They were done, but according to Harri, it was impossible to estimate how far along I was as there was so much swelling in the ankle. Yet he also said that there had been some improvement, and he urged me to continue with the rehabilitation plan.

Instinctively, I knew there had to be a fundamental change in how we were approaching this, despite all the assurances I was receiving. Was I impulsive? Was I trusting my intuition? Maybe both, but definitely the latter. I could sense that my Achilles wasn't really healing. When I heard that Carlos Ávila de Borba was coming to Finland to hold a training camp in Kuopio, I immediately booked my flight. I had gotten to know Carlos in California when I was still being coached by Rafael, and I was intrigued. The founder of the Kuopio figure skating club Ulla Papp had met Carlos in the early 2000s in Oberstdorf, where Carlos worked as Carolina Kostner's off-ice trainer. Ulla subsequently invited Carlos to Finland many times and he had often visited Kuopio.

Carlos' coaching has influenced many Finnish athletes, not just figure skaters but also ski jumpers and alpine skiers. I was convinced that Carlos was the only person who could help me. I was impressed with his know-how of the mechanics of the skater's body. Surely, he would be able to evaluate if I was a hypochondriac or if there was a real reason for my pain. When I got to Kuopio, Carlos immediately noticed my limp, even when I just walked across the floor. Carlos declared that there was no way I could start jump practice in that condition and that we would need yet another medical opinion.

And with that began my intense collaboration with Carlos. We started a rehabilitation project together, and it was a big financial investment. Right from the start, Carlos was quite aware of his value. But I was ready to invest money in my health and my career. I believed in Carlos' methods and believed in him as a person. His self-confidence, charisma, and straightforwardness impressed me. Although at times I was taken aback by his highly critical words, I still saw this as one of the characteristics of a successful and demanding coach. That's exactly what I wanted. I also desperately wanted to fix my leg and get back to the intensity of competition. I believed every word Carlos said and jumped into the project full on.

> Having a series of injuries is mentally really tough. It's living with constant fear. What if the injury doesn't heal? I have never in my life seen an athlete who worked as hard as Kiira did during her last rehabilitation period. People sometimes focus on scores and placement, but behind the scenes Kiira was

superhuman when it came to the amount and intensity of training she did. I have never seen anything like it.—Satu Lähteenkorva, psychologist, Kiira's mental coach, 2012–2015

Carlos lived in Munich with his family. His wife Anna managed to get an appointment for me with Hans-Wilhelm Müller-Wohlfahrt, who was the primary doctor for the national German football team and the Bayern Munich team. He was one of the leading sports doctors in the world and had treated many international stars, including Paula Radcliffe, Jürgen Klinsmann, Steven Gerrard, and Usain Bolt, who owed his 100-meter Olympic gold in Rio de Janeiro to Müller-Wohlfahrt.

> Without [Dr. Muller], I would never have been able to enjoy so much success and so many medals. For me, he is without doubt the best sports orthopaedist in the world.—Usain Bolt*

When I walked into Müller-Wohlfahrt's upscale clinic in central Munich in February of 2014, almost six months had passed since I had torn my Achilles. Modern art adorned the walls, thanks to his wife. Also on the wall were the golden spikes donated by Bolt. The 70-year-old doctor stepped into the room. There were three to four parts to his handshake, and I tried to keep up. His charisma shone immediately, and I'll bet his patients get a placebo effect just from being around him. He emanated warmth and care, as if my ailment was now his top priority in the world. He is highly respected in professional sports, and I could see why. When he was examining my calf with his fingers it felt as if he had radar that could "see" the cells and ligaments through the skin.

"If you had attempted just one more major jump, your Achilles tendon would have torn completely," said the German doctor after examining me and looking at the new MRIs.

The rehabilitation hadn't progressed as we had hoped at all. Yes, there was 30 percent of a healthy tendon remaining at the time of the injury, but six months later, the situation was completely unchanged. No wonder it still hurt so much to make jump attempts. All of this became so clear when my new MRIs were examined and interpreted in Germany, something that had been missed in Finland.

---

* https://fcbayern.com/en/news/2020/07/usain-bolt-bono-and-wladimir-klitschko-thank-dr-muller-wohlfahrt; Picture of Kiira with Bolt: https://www.instagram.com/kiira_korpi/p/lxt1KYEASF/.

I'm sure that in Finland they tried to treat me in the best possible way, but the plan put in place by Harri Hakkarainen didn't meet my expectations at all. Maybe I wasn't a priority athlete for him, maybe he had too much work, or maybe he had a difficult life situation at the time. I wasn't sure I was being heard, which is sometimes the case with athletes and their doctors and trainers. Should I have just bluntly said what I thought instead of being so deferential? Should I have said, "Goddammit, Harri, I can't even walk on this leg!" Yes, I should have. But I want to repeat what got me so upset. Why couldn't the right diagnosis have been made in Finland as it was in Germany?

> We didn't want to talk about malpractice at the press conference; it wouldn't have brought Kiira's Achilles back. But if that is the level of care in Finland with the best experts, what is the level in the clubs or in local programs? We can't say that Kiira's career ended with that injury but again we started a fight against time, with a half a year against us, trying to see if the tendon could grow back together or not. It was a very unfortunate thing.—Mikko Luukkaa, manager

Dr. Müller-Wohlfahrt combines homeopathy with traditional medicine. He has gotten a lot of criticism for the homeopathic treatments he practices. He might for instance coat a soccer player's knee with rooster comb extract or honey. In my case, he held back from recommending surgery as long as possible, but his amino acid injections weren't helping enough. Besides, so much dead tissue had already accumulated that it needed to be removed with surgery. In April 2014, Müller-Wohlfahrt's trusted colleague Ulrich Stöckle performed the procedure on my foot. He took some healthy tendon from higher up in my leg and grafted it into the torn area. Finally, seven long months after I tore it, the Achilles tendon started to heal. I demanded that the insurance plan of the Olympic committee cover the 10,000-euro surgery and treatment costs, as I had clear evidence that the treatment and medical advice I had received in Finland had been ineffective.

After the surgery in the spring of 2014, I moved in with Carlos' family in Munich for three months. We started rehabilitation immediately even while my leg would remain in a cast for six more weeks. I walked to my training sessions on crutches. Carlos invented clever strengthening exercises for the pool, the athletics field, the stationary bike, and eventually on the ice. We worked on mobility, balance, motor skills, and deep muscle control. While my tissues were healing steadily, I learned a lot, and I felt I was going in the right direction. Training with Carlos was

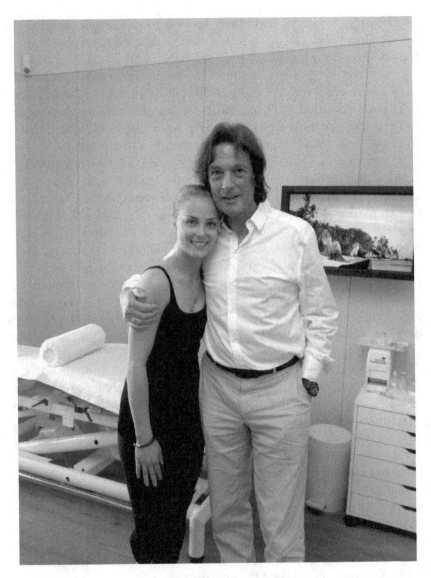

With Dr. Müller-Wohlfahrt.

very intense, even off the ice. We practiced six times a week, many hours a day, just the two of us.

Two months after surgery I got permission from the doctor to get back in the rink. Carlos and I decided to continue training in California but first we stopped over in Toronto where Shae-Lynn was creating a new program for me. From there we flew to Los Angeles to practice with Rafael's team. The dynamic between Carlos and Rafael had shifted. Carlos was now kind of my primary coach and so their roles were reversed. For this reason and others, the arrangement did not work out. My leg wasn't recovered enough to fully take advantage of Rafael's jump routines. I returned to Europe with Carlos, this time to Oberstdorf, Germany, where there was a lot of ice time available. We continued to train and work closely together throughout the fall of 2014.

That year, on December 6, Finland's independence day, and eight months after my Achilles surgery, I won the international Golden Spin competition in Zagreb. This was in the same arena where I had started my international competitive career at the age of 11 under the influence of a lemon soda sugar rush. This was my first win in two years, and my score was high enough to qualify once more to represent Finland at the European and world championships. This was also the first time Carlos stood rinkside as my coach. The last few incredibly painful months had paid off, at least to get me to *this* stage. A few weeks later at the Finnish championships in Tikkurila I won gold with a big 11-point gap over the second-place finisher in what turned out to be my last Finnish championship.

From outside, everything seemed to be going well. I couldn't bask in the Finnish gold. I now had to immediately do a grueling five-day training camp in Vierumäki because we needed to get ready for the European championships coming up in January, in Stockholm. My new mental coach and psychologist, Satu Lähteenkorva, sat in the locker room with me and saw my tears. Satu had been waiting for me to come to Finland so she could see me train with Carlos. I had met Satu once, about two years earlier, when I was still living and practicing in Tampere. Satu was there working with young Tappara skaters and happened to see me break down during training then, too, crying hysterically because nothing went right that day. Now, two years later, here I was in tears once again.

"It's nothing. It's just that I've been working so intensively with Carlos for five days," I explained through my tears.

Satu didn't buy my explanation. As we started to chat quietly, she sensed something wasn't right. Satu was interested in me as a whole person, not just as an athlete, and from that moment we began our wonderful work together, work that continued long after the end of my competitive career.

Satu's careful observation of my practice sessions with Carlos had confirmed her opinion. Carlos wasn't very pleased with Satu's presence and was offended by some of the questions she had for us. Carlos later said to me that it was fine if I needed the help of a psychologist but he definitely didn't.

> An alcoholic can't get better unless they recognize there's a problem. A workaholic won't make a change if they insist that they are stronger than anyone around them. Only once a person admits to themselves the clear signs of exhaustion will that person take action. When someone is suffering in this way, one of the first things to go is their capacity for good judgment.—Satu Lähteenkorva, psychologist, Kiira's mental coach, 2012–2015

Another time I was in the cafeteria with Satu and suddenly broke down again, and again I came up with some excuse. I always did. It's not that I didn't notice the clear signs of extreme exhaustion. With Carlos' incredibly rigorous plan I was more fatigued than ever, but I was determined *not* to let my feelings get in the way of the training. I knew that the most important competitions of the season, the European and world championships, were still ahead. I convinced myself that I just needed to be tougher, not give up. Satu did not like the whole scenario and sensed that the coaching relationship with Carlos didn't improve my well-being—quite the opposite. But in my state of mind at that time, my judgment was impaired. I couldn't "hear" what Satu was saying. I also didn't hear what my own body was telling me. I refused to acknowledge my exhaustion and the crippling anxiety because I hadn't yet reached my goal. I had one thought that dominated my entire being: I wanted to achieve something great.

≈ 20 ≈

"You are no longer good for me"

It has been unsettling to look back and realize what a bad state I was in during the spring of 2015. I didn't realize it myself at the time. The exhaustion and the increasingly challenging coaching relationship with Carlos was leading to a crisis that was more serious than anything I had experienced in my entire life.

After the tears dried in Vierumäki, I pushed through to the European championships in Stockholm at the end of January. I had to quit the competition after the short program due to a stomach bug, my body's way of slamming on the brakes. But my mind didn't agree with my body. I didn't want to stop. I longed for success. I persuaded myself to keep training under Carlos' watchful eye. I was desperate to insert more difficulty into my programs before March, when I would head to the world championships in Shanghai. That was going to happen no matter what.

I was increasingly irritated by Carlos and his comments. Meanwhile, my Achilles was still healing. I was emotionally catatonic, as if I was carrying a heavy weight. In retrospect, what happened at the Shanghai world championships was inevitable, the complete breakdown of a skater's body and psychological self—and I felt that I was watching the disaster from the outside. This was in a way a spiritual experience. I can say that this experience had a revolutionary effect on my thinking. After Shanghai, something was dying inside, but something else was becoming ever more alive. I was past the point of wondering whether my career was over or not. I needed to think thoroughly about who I was, what I wanted to be, and who I *didn't* want to be. I felt split in two—one part of me tried to convince myself to continue training, while a deep and wordless intuition was urging me to let go. This process took many months, and there were many different stages on this journey.

20. *"You are no longer good for me"*

A human being is really magnificent and it moves me how wonderfully we are built. When someone is as tired as Kiira was, the mind starts to protect the person and shows them that that's enough. Humans are so insanely beautiful.—Satu Lähteenkorva, psychologist

Carlos, my goals haven't changed. I still want to become the best figure skater in the world.—Email to Carlos, April 16, 2015

Gearing up for the next season began immediately after the huge disappointment in China. I dashed off an email to Carlos telling him that my goals remained the same. I wanted to become the best figure skater in the world. I had dreamed of this since I was eight years old when I got those VHS tapes and first saw Michelle Kwan skate. My dream was nourished by my early successes, then became a more concrete goal, but then morphed into an obsession. What started so innocently became an irrational belief that my life would be perfect *if only* I could reach the top. In Shanghai, even after my spectacular collision with reality, I refused to believe that it was the end. The train was still speeding down the tracks. And I still wanted to work with Carlos even though I knew our relationship was terrible—simply because I felt there was no other way to achieve my dream. I returned to Finland from the world championships at the end of March. I reserved my flight to Oberstdorf, Germany, for April 19 to resume training, but first Arthur and I decided to spend two weeks in the Canary Islands.

I was in no state to enjoy our vacation. My mind was buzzing every moment with all the anxieties about the future. Nothing could soothe or relax me, not the massages, not the chocolate treatments, and not even the lovely company. Poor Arthur had to tolerate a constantly ruminating girlfriend. At the time I didn't understand that I was having symptoms of complex PTSD (post-traumatic stress disorder). PTSD usually results from a traumatic event, such as a natural disaster or car accident, but complex PTSD (C-PTSD) results from repeated trauma over months or years rather than a single event. For me, the repeated trauma I had endured in skating and childhood had left a huge mark in my nervous system.

During our time together in the Canary Islands I realized that I couldn't stand the very thought of going back to Germany to train with Carlos. It gave me so much anxiety that I would have had a panic attack on the plane. I just needed more time to pull myself together.

Carlos, I have clear symptoms of burn out. I need a bit more time to rest. We can maybe start a week later than planned. I will keep myself in good physical condition all the time. I haven't been myself lately, but I'm not blaming anyone for this.

In fact, his coaching style was too much for me. I felt overwhelmed and depleted. I needed more space to breathe. I wrote to him with some new ideas I had for redesigning our work plan. I suggested that I be in charge of my own practice on weekends. I thought he'd like this idea since he had family in Oberstdorf and could even head off to Munich to be with his wife on weekends. I also proposed that I would fly in more members of my team, specifically my mental coach Satu and my physical therapist Jarmo Ahonen. Carlos agreed that a bigger team would be good, but he also made it very clear that the new arrangement would not mean that he would be paid any less.

Carlos had been talking about extending his contract very early in our relationship, around the time of the Finnish championships in December of the previous year, about halfway through the season. He reminded me about it regularly. I paid Carlos a monthly salary of thousands of euros for our first season together, an arrangement that was very rare in figure skating. I'm sure no club coach in Finland earns anything close to that amount. Carlos' only full-time client was me, but in the Finnish club, coaches might have tens or hundreds skaters under their care. According to Carlos he was not charging me *enough* for his work. For the next season he would want a raise, the same amount he was getting from his former coachee in Japan. This meant practically doubling his salary. The contract negotiations started to open my eyes to Carlos' motives. I got the feeling that money was the biggest reason Carlos still wanted to be part of my project.

Mikko helped me put together what I thought was a reasonable counteroffer, which was still about triple that of an average income in Finland, and on top of that we proposed bonuses for successful outcomes. I thought that was more than generous, and I did have to start being careful with my financial situation. Support from my sponsors was stagnating, and the coaching grants from the federation and the Olympic committee were tiny in comparison with the numbers Carlos was asking for.

Carlos' response was blunt. He was not interested in tying any part of his compensation to my performance. Well, that didn't show much confidence in me! He also expressed the belief that he was already doing all he could and that he wasn't going to be the one to suffer just because I thought the cost was too high.

20. *"You are no longer good for me"*

We could not reach an agreement. Carlos stuck to his salary request and had no interest in performance-based bonuses. He wanted as small a risk as possible with as big a reward as possible. Looking at the situation purely from a business point of view, I would say that Carlos' value wasn't close to the six-figure annual salary he demanded. At that price, I could have flown my choreographer Shae-Lynn and Jami to Germany many times and would have received a much more well-rounded training.

The breakdown in negotiations was a blessing in disguise. I have often thought about what would have happened if Carlos had agreed to our offer. Would I have jumped once more into the same rat race? Would I have continued to search desperately for fulfillment and perfection? I believe that the whole agonizing process of negotiating with Carlos led to some healthy changes in me in the spring of 2015. It was meant to go like this.

> The trust between Carlos and Kiira was built during Kiira's rehabilitation period. In Oberstdorf the rhythm, however, changed radically. Carlos had such a comprehensive touch with coaching that it reached everything from breakfast to evening prayers. No adult could handle such a coaching relationship. Not even in a relationship are the couple together so tightly all the time. Carlos has serious achievements, from coaching world champions to Olympic medalists, but the personas of Carlos and Kiira didn't fit together in the long run.—Mikko Luukkaa, manager

I'm thankful to Carlos for a lot of things. He and his wife Anna introduced me to Müller-Wohlfahrt's practice. Also, Carlos and Anna took me warmly into their home during my rehabilitation period. At first, I believed in Carlos' coaching philosophy and trusted his expertise. I admired his confidence, and he was very persuasive as well, maybe too persuasive.

A serious problem was that he started to criticize me not only as an athlete but also as a person, in a way that was frightening. And an equally serious problem was that I didn't have the ability to stand up for myself. Around Carlos I couldn't be fully myself. I tried to be what he wanted me to be. I think he was insecure and needed to pick others apart, but he was able to distract me from noticing this with his charisma and the momentum of the work. I ended up feeling manipulated. I'm very sad that I allowed myself to lose some of my own power and my own voice, which, to be honest, had already been kind of restricted since childhood, and that's why I believe I unconsciously attracted overcontrolling people and relationships in my life again and again.

Kiira Korpi

What started as a productive relationship between two highly demanding perfectionists turned out to be not such a good combo after all. I wrote Carlos a letter because I needed to express my thoughts and have a release for my feelings. I never sent that letter.

Carlos,

I'm sad that things ended up this way. I didn't realize before Shanghai how badly I was feeling mentally and how much hidden frustration I had with you. Our intensive work unknowingly resulted in a situation where I felt something was wrong with me as a person. I believed that if I didn't change as a person, I couldn't be a good skater. I don't believe that anymore. Although I come from Finland and although I am friendly towards others, I can still be a great skater. Actually I want people to remember me as a good person, not just as a great skater. I trusted my career and even my life in your hands and believed in you. I admired you as a person, too. I probably spent more time in one and half years with you than I have spent with Arthur during our whole relationship. You were always polite, friendly, and you charmed my family. You have a lovely wife Anna and I admired your relationship. It looked like you knew how a happy life is built. I was sure that you are a person whom I wanted to have as a friend and a mentor after my skating career was over. I'm really happy that I got to work with you. I'm also really happy that I don't need to work with you anymore. You are no longer good for me. I know you didn't hurt me on purpose, you did it to hide your own insecurities and weaknesses. That's what we all do. We all sometimes are fearful, weak and fragile. I wish you all the best, I don't regret anything. We both tried our best and this is the point it took us to.

—Kiira

⇛ 21 ⇚

From Kiira to Kiira

I was relieved that the coaching relationship with Carlos was over, but now I was deeply confused, uncertain. My whole future was open. At the end of April, I spent a few days by myself in Spain because I needed time and space to be alone and think about my situation in peace. I could sense that little by little I was becoming more compassionate toward myself. Writing became more and more important for me and really clarified my thinking. I wrote myself a letter in Malaga on the 27th of April 2015.

This is a letter from the Kiira who's sensitive, vulnerable, uncertain, trusting of others, loving and loved, *the real* Kiira, to that Kiira who's externally successful, beautiful, efficient and high-achieving but who's *not real*.

Dear Kiira,

From a very early age you learned to accomplish things well and efficiently. You were gifted and skillful, you had an amazing memory and capacity to learn. You were also very strong-willed, which enabled you to solve any task if not thanks to your talent then at least thanks to your willpower. You always performed well in school, and in skating, where you started to really succeed when you were about 11 years old.

The fact that you were excellent both in school and in skating became a kind of expectation. Due to your amazing ability to focus and remember, you didn't need to put in a lot of effort, and you still finished high school with a grade average of 9.9 out of 10. Your achievements in school and skating were received positively in your household, but they weren't particularly celebrated either, and you were encouraged to always keep a "low profile" so that you wouldn't appear arrogant. If you did a little worse in a competition or on an exam, you didn't receive any special criticism, but the expectation from yourself, your family, your teachers and coaches was that you'd generally excel.

You didn't strive for perfection, but you got used to the fact you had to outperform. At home, at the ice rink and overall in your culture it was

157

common to value people based on their work performance and external success. Probably that's why you also started thinking that if you got a particular achievement only then could you be happy with yourself.

The first time you experienced a serious burnout you were in your senior year of high school. You had just competed at the Olympics, you handled the sudden publicity and sponsorship commitments (without a manager) and "on the side" went to high school like everyone else. No wonder you exhausted yourself, but at that moment you couldn't realize why you were so tired, since you had always done everything without huge problems. You'll always remember the day a journalist called you and asked you to take part in a short radio interview. You looked at your absolutely crammed calendar and responded that you have a one-hour break on Friday between school and training, so you could just squeeze in the 30-minute interview.

Dear Kiira, although you learned over the years to reduce your school and workload, you hired a manager and learned to say no to some things, your subconscious desire to achieve acceptance from yourself and others based on your performance didn't go away. You knew that it's important to have a life outside of skating, and not to build your sense of self only based on skating, but maybe when you're so young it's difficult to make profound changes or know the deepest essence of your being. Therefore, the exhaustion always returned. And that's why it didn't take long even after a big win until the nagging voice inside you would return and say that "this is not enough" and you moved on towards the next challenge and goal.

When you were battling your Achilles tendon injury for a few years and weren't sure if it would ever get better, you had to face the question of how it would feel to live a life without skating. But you wanted to get your foot fixed and keep going, because the inner fire was still so strong and you had a feeling that you hadn't reached your full potential as a skater yet. Before that your decision to change coaches (first ever in your career) had taught you to listen to your own intuition more carefully. Therefore, you had the courage to make brave choices and let go of the negative training environment in America. You moved to Germany to work with a coach believing that training with him would finally be the key to rising to the world's very top.

Unfortunately, or fortunately, life doesn't always go as you plan. Ultimately, the coach seemed to care more about money and his own prestige than you. Although you had learned a tremendous amount from him, working with him started to eat away at your self-confidence. Then there was the incredible pressure to succeed so soon after your serious injuries. Too soon. Once again you totally wore yourself out. You were so drained and mistreated by your coach (and yourself) that after the disastrous world championships you felt completely empty and helpless. That's why you seriously considered and perhaps still consider the future of your skating career and what your values are.

Already during the previous season, you had started to contemplate if competitive sports at the highest level made sense in your case, since it seemed to once again injure your health and the results weren't really all that impressive either. You longed for a deeper sense of meaning for your work. That was a cry for help from me, the real Kiira.

For a long time, you have counted health, love and family as the most important values to you. Also, curiosity about the world and other people, as well as learning new things and personal growth have been high on your list. How well do you think you've succeeded in living up to these values? Well, for one thing, you haven't been very healthy. Obviously, you have loved and been loved by your family and the people closest to you, but have you felt that you can love yourself exactly as you are? Or have you assumed that you can only love yourself "fully" once you've achieved this or that in skating or in other areas in life?

Learning new things and curiosity about the world seem to have stayed also very performance-based in your case. You have tried to develop yourself a lot as a skater to be physically and mentally tougher and stronger, but have you ever considered that your curiosity could be focused towards me, the real you, where you find your weaknesses, but through facing and accepting them you would also uncover your strengths?

The first sports psychologist you ever worked with, not to mention your previous coach, told you that you're too sensitive to be successful in high level sports. Please don't believe them anymore, ok? Your sensitivity, vulnerability and ability to empathize makes you the unique you that you are, and it can be a huge gift in skating as well.

According to me, the real you, you should let go of judging yourself based on your achievements. Only then can you live according to your values and love yourself and others genuinely. The identity you have built upon your accomplishments and performance goals is not real. You know that yourself so well, dear sweet Kiira. I know that throwing yourself into the unknown stream of life is scary, but the Universe or God, or however you wish to call that force that's larger than us, will carry you and has designed your path so there's no point for you to plan it too specifically in advance. The fact that you dare to face your weaknesses and appreciate yourself as you are in any given moment won't be easy or always fun. On the contrary, it will hurt and needs practicing, but it is REAL. And in the end, that's the only thing that matters. So, you might just want to get used to and love your imperfections, because it's a waste of precious time and health to strive for perfection that doesn't exist. Besides, dear Kiira, if you can't learn to love yourself the way you are there's no way you can love others unconditionally, though you might believe that you already can.

Now you must be wondering if you can ever continue to skate at a competitive level if you're not striving to achieve medals so fanatically. You've always thought that an athlete's "task" is to accumulate medals and by doing so also glory for the whole nation. As words of comfort I want to tell you that you can still aim to be the best skater you can ever be and achieve the best results you possibly can. Maybe you'll reach the very top, maybe you won't. But what matters is not so much the results but the reason why you skate. You don't need skating in order to build a strong identity for yourself. You should skate only if your true self wants that. And I know that I want to skate. I feel like it's a gift from the Universe for me in this world through which I can do good for my soul and other people's souls, and inspire young people by my example and perhaps other ways, too.

Dear Kiira. In order for you to end the cycle of overachieving and burning out, and the hollow feeling in the midst of external success, please give me now some time and space to reflect on things and guide you towards the right path. A path where a human being experiences fear, uncertainty, risk, doubt, hesitation, disappointment and sadness, but also true love, acceptance, connection with nature, other people, the Universe, yourself, and most of all, a path where everything is real. That's why it feels so liberating and good to be on that path.

≈ 22 ≈

Breaking into Wholeness

Marjatta is one of the reasons I developed into a good skater, *and* one of the reasons I didn't develop into an even better skater. Marjatta believes that a good life is achieved by constantly outperforming and striving to be the best. Marjatta is my inner judge, not the real me.

Marjatta has expressed herself strongly for years, but it wasn't until the summer of 2015 that I got to know who she really was, a ruthless judge without any compassion. I named her Marjatta because the name helped differentiate Marjatta's and Kiira's thinking models, which were mixed up in my mind. Marjatta would make me go for a run in the evening if I had eaten ice cream at some point during the day. She didn't suggest it—she demanded it. Marjatta thought that a basic Pilates class wasn't challenging enough, even if simply breathing felt like work for me. When I looked in the mirror, Marjatta would say that my skin was too thick, or any number of mean things. No matter how much or little I weighed, she was never content. That summer I started to understand that Marjatta's critical comments about *everything* I did weren't necessarily true, because *she* wasn't true. She was a construct of my mind, a sad little monster—my ego, whom for a long time I mistook for me. Marjatta had nothing to do with my core essence, which goes far beyond any part of my limited mind.

I absolutely needed to see Marjatta's hurtful commentary for what it was. But she had become a loyal companion over the years and in a twisted way I loved her very much. I loved the rush of pleasure when I obeyed her endless commands. When I was able to control and punish myself, it was as if I had taken some sort of drug. Then the inevitable crash would come, and I ended up feeling worse than before, but listening to Marjatta was a deep-seated biological and psychological habit, and it felt almost safer to continue to be cruel to myself rather than compassionate. Thankfully, I was ready to take the risk to lean on love.

I wanted the right to feel I was enough the way I was. Slowly, I forced Marjatta to move over. Not by pushing her back into the darkness, but by shedding more light and love on her.

I was in a wild whirlpool of emotions in May of 2015. I was getting ready to take my last trip to Germany for the Achilles tendon. I was still officially working with Carlos. When I got to Munich, I didn't contact him. I needed to be alone. I made this decision to honor my own well-being. I was locked in a tremendous battle with Marjatta and thinking about my future. After examining my foot, the doctor assured me there was no reason I could not continue to compete. He said I was at a prime age as a figure skater. Well, I wasn't convinced about that, but I was actually still planning to go to Toronto in June to create a new program with the wonderful Shae-Lynn. Even if my competitive career were to end, the choreography we'd create would be a good show piece.

After my last world championships, I had only hit the ice a few times to do some comfortable edges and easy gliding. I usually didn't last long out there. One time I was only on the ice for five minutes before I had to head back to the locker room, where I would cry hysterically. Those tears had built up inside me for years. In that transformational time, Marjatta sometimes managed to force me to do a short workout, but otherwise my training was minimal. One day my dad called and asked if I had done any exercise, even jogging.

"I have taken some walks."

"When will you start to go for runs?"

"I don't know," I replied, although I wanted to shout, *"Maybe never!!!!!"* When I hung up, I cried my eyes out. That spring there was plenty of crying. Dad only meant well. But I was hurt when even my own parents saw me first as a skater and not as a person. Why did it have to be like that?

I felt so utterly broken inside. I was exhausted, totally exhausted, and more than anything I longed to return to being a functioning, good human being. Meetings and discussions with my mental coach Satu were vital. Satu was ideal because she was detached enough from my closest circle of people, and she was very professional and empathic. Satu used her skills wisely, allowing me to fully express what was going on inside. I blurted out all my feelings to her. She didn't judge and wasn't horrified. Sometimes she was firm with me but gave me the space to dismantle my unhealthy thought patterns, to really *see* them in the harsh yet liberating light of honest self-discovery.

22. *Breaking into Wholeness*

I faced the realization of how ruthless and insensitive I had been toward myself and toward the people in my life during those years when I was passionately pursuing my career goals; I saw how anxiety and over-thinking had completely taken over my mind; how negatively I talked to myself. I saw that mentally I was in really bad shape. Now I understood that when I hit the ice in Shanghai, I had been psychologically paralyzed.

I was incomplete and imperfect. But now my incompleteness and imperfection were no longer cause for searing self-criticism, at least not all the time. I was at a place from where I could start again, broken but fully alive, broken but true to myself—for once. I was irritated at how polished my public image had become, a Kiira who was free of the sad-ness, fear, disappointment, and anxiety that everyone feels at some point in their lives, that the real Kiira felt so often. I had allowed others to mis-treat me, and I had been so cruel to myself that the negative and scary feelings had built up tremendously. But not the public Kiira! Out there I was still the breezy, successful Kiira Korpi. I felt a powerful urge to share a truer image. I started posting some pictures and texts on social media where I think people could see a few more of the rough edges, where I showed more vulnerability than I had ever shown. That was hard for me to do.

I started to accept the idea that I might not get back into training anytime soon. I accepted the possibility that a comeback would never happen. I trusted my unconscious and higher knowing, and I trusted that this deeper part of me was moving things along at the right speed; I wanted to live strongly and follow my intuition without forcing myself into anything. I broke my protective barriers down one by one and dove deeper into myself. I believed that beneath it all, something good, beau-tiful, and real would emerge.

According to Satu, I was making progress that summer; I sounded less tense. I could feel in my gut that I was going in the right direc-tion although exactly where was unclear. There were times when I just wanted to get out on ice and see how it felt. Back in Finland I headed out with my skates a couple of times, just to glide around. I didn't do this to improve or challenge myself or work toward a medal. Instead, I listened carefully to hear if the ice was truly calling me. And when I worked with Shae in Toronto to create that new program, I felt empowered, as I always did with her. Just playing around on the ice with Shae imme-diately made me feel better. The fear and uncertainty about the future were still with me, but so was a growing feeling of trust and optimism.

Kiira Korpi

In June I started a new kind of diary, a journal of gratitude. I listed things to be grateful for and things that brought me joy each day. The idea of listing positive things was something I had done for the first time about ten years earlier when the *Positiivarit* media chose me as the most positive Finn of 2006. Mostly my journals were full of self-doubt, fear, and dreams of ever-higher goals. In this new time, Satu agreed that the gratitude diary was a good idea. The memory of things that bring you joy might completely disappear from the mind of an exhausted and depressed person. With daily attention, these positive feelings could be encouraged back out on the surface.

1. *I woke up next to Arthur and we listened to music together in the morning.*
2. *I got to have a nice dinner with Arthur's work friends and we laughed until we cried when Paolo started cracking jokes.*
3. *I'm travelling pleasantly on a train to Trento and I get to watch the landscape, read, and just kick back.*
4. *This will be a fun day. I will meet a new coach, maybe someone I'll be working with. I don't know how that will turn out but I'll accept everything that comes my way with an open mind.*

The dead end with Carlos had forced me to think about other coaching possibilities—that is, if I were to continue my career. In Europe the options were limited, and the only good option I could imagine at the time was to be coached by Franca Bianconi, in Italy, and I even took a trip down there to meet her. It looked like it might have been a good match. But inside, momentum toward ending my career had progressed too far. I still loved skating, I loved the floating feel of a glide, but goal-oriented training didn't feel meaningful anymore. By the end of June 2015 my diary pages already showed signs of letting go.

28th June 2015: *I know that my life's meaning is to be a person who loves herself and others for their humanity, not for their accomplishments or skills. I want to give myself mercy and time, and not to force things. Good things happen when I let go of the obsessive reaching after them. I have learned a lot. I don't need to explain to anyone, not even myself, why I skate. I hope that by taking this path I could make the world a little more beautiful and humane through my skating. For this reason I want to have an open heart, to lean on the uncertainty of life, to go towards my fear. Even if I fail, I would still succeed, because I would dare to be vulnerable and respect my body and my mind so much that I wouldn't push it over its natural limits.*

It might be that I can't compete with the younger, more technical skaters, but my main goal isn't competing but performing from the bottom of my

heart, living courageously, and touching people. I can go for a jog or prac-
tice if I really want to but these days have been really tough, and it simply
feels better to have mercy and rest. Rest in the moment, work through my
thoughts, release the sadness, anger, and all the shit that has been piling up
throughout the years. That, if anything, is something that does good! Better
than any training in the world because then I am completely true to myself
and others.

During the past few days I have also gotten to experience beautiful things,
unbelievable freedom and peaceful feelings even in the middle of sadness
and pain. I believe that my sadness and anger these days is no longer aimed
at any one person or thing, I'm just sad about the life I failed to live fully and
how hard I have been on myself and also how I have let others treat me so
badly. I'm going to find out if it's possible to suspend my studies and think
about something that really interests me.

I have started to become interested in organic physical movements that
are not forced, but I will work according to how my body feels each day and
strengthen it from the inside out. I want to be strong inside. I will respect my
body even if I am not able to perform a certain movement. I will try to be
more merciful to my body. I will thank my sore back, which has held up so
long even though I have abused it by mentally blocking out weaknesses and
storing them partly in my body. My dear little left Achilles and calf have had
such a hard time, and now they need love and care and strengthening on
their own terms.

My body is so wise, but of course the life lived leaves marks and scars. From
here on out I want to treat it with respect, by training within the limits it sets
and by carrying it with pride. I have needed to face some difficult experiences
from childhood and youth, to let out a lot of anger, pain and grief. There have
been times when even breathing has felt heavy, but slowly my protective bar-
rier is starting to break down and light shines through more and more.

Four months had passed since the events of Shanghai. Emotionally,
I had matured a lot, but I still had a lot of questions. The coaching situation was up in the air. The continuation of my whole career was up in the
air. I continued meeting with Satu and sought out emotionally and spiritually nourishing literature. I had already been reading a lot during the
spring, for example, Tommy Hellsten's and Brené Brown's work, which
reassured me, helped me feel that I'm not alone with my anxiety and I'm
valuable just the way I am.

I also looked for peer support in athletes' biographies and read the
swimmer Ian Thorpe's and hurdler Manuela Bosco's stories. Although I
had never met Manuela, she radiated good energy. I felt we had similar
struggles at the end of our sports careers. I had burned out by believing
that I could only find meaning in life through performance. I contacted

her and immediately received a lovely answer. She gave me a reading list she liked, including the magnificent Eckhart Tolle and Marianne Williamson. Tolle's *The Power of Now* was a spiritual awakening. It was as if I was led by destiny to find this book, because deep inside I knew I needed exactly what Tolle was writing about. I had been emotionally and spiritually starved for years, and I drank these books and conversations like they were water, and that water kept me alive and growing.

I started to pay attention to things that I had taken for granted. I observed that gap between an in breath and out breath and noted how my breaths were moved by a force much greater than me. I consciously practiced things that some people might think are absurd: I listened to the pauses/silences in music and in between the sounds of nature. I sat listening to where the siren sounds of a fire truck disappeared. I paid attention to the space between objects in a room that made the room a room. I felt that the whole world was opening in front of me for the first time. How had I never realized how green a tree looked when you keep looking? Or how warm water felt against my skin in the shower. Small things, and yet so essential. Sometimes I felt I was losing consciousness when I lapsed into states of deep peace by staring at some trees in the distance. I wasn't losing myself. Quite the opposite. I was expanding my consciousness by being in states of awareness with no conceptual thinking.

Through my books and sitting in silence I started to understand a little of what had happened to me in Shanghai. When that competition fell apart, my skating identity shattered completely. In the step sequence at the end of the free program, it was as if I was looking at myself from the outside, though I was of course executing those sequences like I had thousands of times before. I was "me" and "not me" at the same time. In that moment I tore away from an identity that I had built over many years. It was like a psychological near-death experience. I had always been Kiira Korpi, the figure skater. But if that identity is dismantled, what remains? What if I just left my mind next to my shoes in the foyer and just kept being?

One day I called Jami. He was someone I trusted. I had asked him to take on a bigger role on my coaching team, and we had drawn up a detailed off-ice training plan. But then came a visceral feeling. Something had shifted, forever. I said the words.

"Jami, hey, I'm full of energy but training doesn't just work. I can't do these planned practices."

"Sounds very clear. It's OK, Kiira, it's absolutely fine."

"Exactly. It's absolutely fine."

That was the moment. I didn't need to spell it out. Jami knew what I meant. I couldn't ramp up to systematic training once more. My body wouldn't move out the door even when my mind was still stubbornly pushing me to keep going. I had practiced and lived a scheduled life for 15 years and now I was done. I was done. By mid–July the final decision was made. My competitive career would come to a close.

The feeling became so strong and clear that I didn't need to hear what anyone else had to say. I knew what I was doing. Skating would always be a part of my life. I still loved the feeling on the ice, that sensation of being alive on the edge of your blades. So why did I want to let go of something I love, something that so strongly feels like my own element and my unique way of expressing myself? It took time to see that skating could and would take on a new form and meaning. The principle that guided my decision-making then has been useful later on in life when I have made other big decisions. Often, the right decision, matured gradually by the guidance of your heart, is accompanied by a strong sense of peace and doesn't need to be verified or explained to anyone. A thousand people could try to prove your decision wrong, but you won't budge. You know in your bones what's right for you.

> Kiira definitely went to her limits. Exploring your own limits is the essence of competitive sports, although the athletes' performances are compared with one another. An athlete accumulates great amounts of self-knowledge through this exploration. Kiira's world view is completely different from what it would have been had she just kept on doing things here in Tampere.—Rauno Korpi, father

> Kiira's career is wonderful, absolutely glorious. It is a career of a star in Finnish figure skating. What needs to be learned from it is to get to know the athlete's temperament better and to head off any troubles in time.—Anuliisa Uotila, figure skating coach and national team head coach, 2002–2012

It's too easy in hindsight to say that the phone call to Jami marked the moment when I brought my competitive career to a close, but this moment was preceded by an internal process of nearly four months, a time when I let the pieces of my mind-made identity fall away one by one.

The decision was hard on my mom, as her identity had become tied to my skating success. I think that in the beginning she thought I would still change my mind. Even harder for her seemed to be my decision to halt my university studies in Finland, which, by the way, are free to everyone in the country. She was very disappointed about that. I understood her reaction because education was very important for her generation. As a teacher, she had always highlighted the importance of education to me and Petra. Still, it was painful and all too familiar to have my mom try to control my life. This time I wasn't going to be crushed under her will—not even when she ferociously tried to get me to at least complete the bachelor's degree in economics by trying to make me feel guilty, saying how much they had sacrificed for my career. According to her, finishing my studies was something I owed *them*. If I didn't go along with that, I was an ungrateful child. I stayed in my own truth and told her I couldn't go for a degree just to make her happy. In fact, I no longer wanted to do anything in life just to fulfill someone else's expectations of me. To say the least, it felt uncomfortable to stand up against my own dear mom, but by being steady and clear about my decisions, I was gaining back my own voice and power.

The Fullness of Emptiness

I stand motionless in the final position. The music has stopped, but it feels like I'm still moving through space. The moment is so quiet and empty, and yet so full. The crowd is roaring and applauding; I have the feeling that I've been able to give them something special. The scores don't cross my mind; the analyzing thoughts will hit me soon enough. I glide back to my coach and hug her. I see and sense her reactions, and now my mind begins to evaluate the program one element at a time. I fixate on shortcomings and imperfections. Did the spins really go that well after all, were the landings of the jumps clean, did I manage to stay present in my interpretation? How high can I place with this program?

But before all that I have lived a moment in ecstasy. How can anyone live without something like this? There's no better feeling than this. Before the thoughts come stomping back in, for just a second, I'm filled with utter peace and fulfillment.

⇌ 23 ⇋

Surrender to Life

A completely squeezed out sponge. Every single drop, squeezed out and squeezed again so that absolutely nothing is left within it. That's how I felt after the world championship catastrophe. But somehow a sponge always reopens bit by bit and becomes itself again.

The months that I lived through after the Shanghai competition up to the moment of my big decision felt like a very long time. A lot was happening inside of me. My defenses started to crumble away. I began to trust that I didn't need to know the exact schedule for the next day or even today. I was learning that I didn't need to base my life on competing for prizes and recognition, that I didn't need to be the best of the best, and that my self-esteem does not depend on outward success or fulfilling the expectations of others. It's enough that I breathe, that I am.

For about 20 years I had focused solely on myself as a skater and put sports above almost everything else. That made me miss so much of the loveliness that surrounded me all along—all the small moments and encounters. Finally I had more space in my mind and in my heart to stop and listen, to wonder, to breathe, and to appreciate the people around me in all their complexity and benevolence. I mourned for what I'd missed, but I wondered. Was my behavior normal in elite sports? To be ruthless with myself, to be so uncompromising? Can the top be reached any other way? These questions started to fade, and the regret started to fade. In this new phase of my life, I started to see so many possibilities, gradually reclaiming all the strength and love that had been inside and around me.

> After retiring from competitive skating, Kiira has clearly thought a lot about the future. A strong concept of freedom radiates from her. Kiira is no longer living only to satisfy the needs of others. —Rauno Korpi, father

New thinking, new places. In the fall of 2015, I moved to Milan to live with Arthur. I immediately fell in love with the city. Our neighborhood by the old town was delightful. In the café next to our apartment nobody ever took their morning coffee to go. People used to stand at the bar and drink their cappuccino or macchiato from beautiful little porcelain cups while exchanging pleasantries with the barista or the person next to them. I attended an intensive Italian language course, but my best Italian teacher was Angela, the janitor of our building. She loved to share all the latest gossip of the neighborhood. I was so happy to practice my Italian with her that I didn't care even if most of what she said went over my head. I treasured my time in Milano, exploring the beautiful parks, getting into the architecture and history of the city. I felt Italians really know how to enjoy life, but maybe that was because I was able to enjoy life, too. *Finalmente*!

I had started to feel really at home in Milan when Arthur received an excellent work offer from Tom Ford in New York. We moved to Manhattan in the summer of 2016. At first, I missed the neighborhood and the community we had had in Milano. I was also much further away from Finland's breathtaking natural spaces and all the people who are so dear to me there. But then New York City started to work its magic. I got used to living on the same block as the Empire State Building, and like many people before me, I found that New York City spoke to me. In a way, being a stranger to New York was easier than I thought because the city seems to embrace people of different cultures and from different backgrounds. But I admit that it took me almost two years before I truly started to find a balanced daily life in this endlessly energetic city. To maintain that balance as a highly sensitive person is a constant work in progress.

Next to our first apartment in New York was a church where the author and spiritual teacher Marianne Williamson held lectures. Her writings, among others, had led me out of my old life and into the new, and there she was, just down the street. I no longer think that these fortunate intersections of people and ideas are coincidental.

I was still on the move. Almost immediately after retiring from competition, I started performing in various shows around the world. In Milano I found a good training space, and I practiced my show programs almost daily. In New York City, I also found my way to a rink, and my visa allowed me to perform in skating shows in the United States. In addition to the shows, I began coaching skaters of different ages, from

Arthur and me in our new hometown—New York City, 2017.

seven to 60. I also choreographed competition programs for some Finnish skaters and did TV work. I was a judge for one season on Finland's *Dancing with the Stars.* In the spring of 2016, I took part in a Finnish musical theater production. It was a fun experience and my first time performing on inline roller skates on stage.

Kiira Korpi

It's difficult for me to imagine Kiira in a state that she is just experimenting and not doing anything goal oriented. I don't believe it will happen. Ambition, will, skill, and intelligence are still in Kiira.—Brita Korpi, mother

In February 2018 I traveled to Copenhagen. I had been invited to co-host Discovery Finland's live Olympic shows every night with Juhani Henriksson and Sami Hedberg. The filming took place over a two-week period in Denmark where Discovery's main studios are located. The role was new for me and sounded interesting. Two days before the first live show the whole team was sitting down to a meal. Suddenly my hands started to sweat, and my breathing came hard. The sensations in my body were overwhelming. I had a powerful urge to get up and leave. I was having a panic attack.

I needed to know why this happened. I had never experienced anything like it, except maybe in Shanghai. I mentioned it right away to the producer and called my psychologist Satu. Satu thought that the panic attack might have been caused by the stress of the new assignment. To be fair, I had already arrived in Denmark a bit shaky from a bachelorette party in Lapland that lasted for days. Alcohol can apparently be a triggering factor for panic attacks, and clearly, I can't hold my alcohol. With the help of some medication, I got a grip on myself and went through

Performing at a skating show in Tallinn, 2015 (Elina Paasonen / Aamulehti).

with the Olympic broadcasts. I think they went well. I had been acting positive and happy all my life, so it was a useful skill in a situation where my insides were stormy and confusing. I'll bet that viewers had no idea I had been on the verge of falling apart.

It took me months to feel more stable again. After returning to New York, I couldn't go to cafeterias or restaurants for many weeks as the noise was cuttingly loud. My senses were still raw and heightened. I couldn't watch any scary news or anything like that as my nervous system would get hyper triggered. Only several months later when I started to work with a therapist did I come to gain some understanding that my issues weren't "only" due to a panic disorder and stress, but that I had been suffering from complex PTSD for years. In Copenhagen the symptoms had flared up to a whole new level. When I had to go on the air to comment on and show my excitement for Olympic sports, the very thing that broke me, I couldn't handle it. The most intense nightmares I've ever experienced were in Denmark. I've had those a lot in my life (sometimes still do), and they are often about skating poorly, being late, not being ready or willing to go compete, or being shamed for gaining weight, and many more! But in Denmark the dreams were more intense. One night, I dreamed I was dying. I had to

Skating as the legendary Sonia Henie in 2017 (Elina Paasonen / Aamulehti).

vigorously shake my body in bed as I tried to desperately pull myself out of it.

In Copenhagen, I believed I was expected to be excited about the race for the medals, I was supposed to sympathize with heartbreaking failures and become super excited about those joyful moments of victory, but the whole time I was carrying on an internal dialogue, wondering about the value of sports at that level. When I did those Olympic broadcasts, I was so fearful for my sanity. It was hard to look at my own face in the mirror. It felt like I wasn't really there, like my whole energetic being was beside me, not embodied inside myself. The worst thing about all this was the intense feeling that I and the whole world were in a dream. Later I learned that intense anxiety can cause derealization, where people and things around you seem unreal, and depersonalization, where you have recurrent feelings of being detached from your body or mind, usually accompanied with a feeling that you are watching yourself from the outside.

After almost three years since retiring from competition, I didn't admit to myself that I needed a much more wholesome routine in my life. I needed to settle down, but instead, those three years had been almost as hectic and as rootless as when I was competing. The change had to be more total. Now I yearned to be in New York City more. From the day we moved there, there had been a big question in my mind. How long would we stay? When would I go back to Europe? With all my traveling and thinking and wondering, Arthur also seemed annoyed that I always kept one foot in Europe.

When I thought about what I could do in New York City, studying psychology emerged as an obvious option. I was amazed that I hadn't thought about it earlier even though it had been in front of me the whole time. The more I have encountered challenges of the mind, the more my desire to help others has grown. I'm interested in how the brain, mind, and awareness work. I know firsthand that change does not come easy. It needs a nudge or even a shove. The panic attack was yet another crisis and mental awakening I needed because it put me face to face with my own fears and made me ask important questions. How can I connect more deeply with others, my true self and the natural world? What is the real purpose of my life?

So I wrote the first CV of my life and applied for university. In the fall of 2018, I started liberal arts studies at The New School in Manhattan. Earlier that spring I had already started a six-month course in applied positive psychology at the Flourishing Center in New York City. I'm especially interested in that field of psychology that helps people to uncover their strengths, values and purpose in life.

> I hope that Kiira finds a place to settle. She has been running around the world for so long. Kiira clearly already has an idea of a family and children.—Petra Korpi, older sister

Ice is my element. Gliding gives me an ethereal feeling that I have always loved and will always love. Even during the toughest times, there was always that spark in me when I got to go on the ice, to glide and move to the music. I love the complete immersion in it. It was painful to differentiate in my mind which part of skating I loved and which part I hated. Eventually I understood that it isn't about what I'm doing, rather *how* and *why* I'm doing it. Skating remains a big part of my life as I have now transitioned into coaching and creating art with my ice skates or roller skates, but it's not the basis of my whole identity anymore; it's rather a wonderful extension of it.

> Although figure skating is an individual sport and requires self-centeredness, Kiira has always been a generous young woman. She is considerate and wants to help others. I'm proud of her as a father. Through many difficulties, Kiira has developed a positive attitude—nothing has come for free for her, except perhaps inheriting her mom's beauty.—Rauno Korpi, father

Maybe I could have made it through my career with less suffering, and sometimes I feel that it's really difficult to forgive myself and others. Yet, deep down I strongly believe that this is how my life path was meant to go. I have even mentally thanked all those people (including myself) whom I allowed to abuse me, because those lessons have shaped me into the person and coach I am today. I know in my bones what kind of a coach I want to be and what kind of a coach I absolutely do not want to be. I've been lucky to experience both ends of the spectrum—coaching through sheer fear and coaching through pure love. I know firsthand how devastating the effects of the first one can be and how magnificently transformative and healing the effects of the latter can be.

What about Marjatta? Where did she go and how is she doing? Marjatta hasn't left me completely. My aim is that we two to live in peace. I've respectfully and firmly asked Marjatta to retire from the advisory board of my mind and make room for new forces to take charge. I thank her for her service and ask her to rest.

At a spring show with Tappara kids.

It's clear to see that now Kiira does things with foresight and with attention to her wellbeing. When the athlete's career is over, the whole basis of their life drops off and the happiness with self is lost. All of a sudden no one tells the athlete what to do. I'm a bit sad how in Finland we don't adequately deal with the challenges of retirement for athletes. Many people are left completely alone and it's horrible.—Satu Lähteenkorva, psychologist

The definition of success has changed for me so much. What do you do with external success, whether it's medals, wins, money, or whatever, if the success doesn't bring inner peace? For me it didn't. I'm not saying that external, material success doesn't have a big value—it absolutely does—but true, wholesome success, for me, at least, springs from the inside out! It means that my actions, thoughts, and emotions are aligned, and I achieve external success as a wonderful and essential byproduct of living such a rich and balanced life internally.

The sponge has returned to its former shape, but not the same as it was before. I have needed to surrender many times and in many ways and to be humble in front of the mystery we call life. I have taken responsibility for my own thoughts and feelings and for the kind of energy I carry and let inside me and share with others. I still struggle with revealing my weaknesses at times, and I imagine it will be a lifelong practice for me like it is for most people I know. Ultimately, I believe that we are all here to be human, not perfect. I have broken into wholeness.

What about you?

Epilogue

When a version of this book was originally published in Finland in September 2018, it became a catalyst for a deeper and more public conversation about ethical issues in the Finnish sports system. I quickly found myself growing into the role of a fierce children's rights activist. I have come to know many current and former elite child athletes who have been sexually, physically and/or emotionally mistreated in sports.

To my absolute surprise and dread I found out that the problem is not that the sports authorities don't know about these serious issues concerning child athletes but that they seem to ignore them. There is a clear pattern that investigation of problematic cases and serious action start only after a story has broken to the media. Unfortunately, they often seem to care much more about their image, money and medals than about the health and well-being of children.

When I say "they," I don't mean any specific group of people. Actually, there are many, many justice-loving and children-loving people working in the field of sports. By "they" I mean more the overall limited and fear-based structures and systems that keep these destructive dynamics in place.

The Prevalence of Emotional Abuse in Coach-Athlete Relationships

After my competitive career, I have invested a lot of time in reading about emotional abuse in sports. In the academic research field, it hasn't been studied to date as extensively as sexual and physical abuse in sports, even though it's estimated to be the most frequently experienced form of abuse in the coach-athlete relationship. According to a large-scale study from the UK, emotional abuse (including but not limited to coach-athlete relationships) is experienced by 75 percent of young athletes in organized sports. Preliminary research has reported that nearly 25 percent of competitive athletes suffer from emotionally abusive coaching practices. These are concerning findings that only highlight the urgent need to improve athlete empowerment and safety in organized sports.

Scientifically speaking, emotional abuse can be defined as a pattern of deliberate non-contact behaviors within a critical relationship that has the potential to be harmful. For a coach-athlete relationship to be categorized as emotionally abusive, the potentially harmful behaviors (i.e., spurning, terrorizing, belittling, humiliating, threatening, exploiting, corrupting and denying emotional responsiveness) must form a *pattern of behavior*, and they must occur on *multiple occasions over a period of time*. The behaviors must also occur within a critical relationship in which the coach has substantial influence over the athlete's sense of safety, trust, and fulfillment of physical and emotional needs; the behaviors must be used deliberately by the coach and be intentionally directed at the athlete (the intention to use these behaviors might or might not be to harm); and the harmful behaviors must be noncontact.

Some specific emotionally abusive behaviors in the coach-athlete relationship include verbal behaviors such as degrading remarks, name-calling, threats, and non-verbal behaviors, for instance, throwing athletic equipment in a threatening manner or intentionally ignoring or isolating an athlete. It's likely that these abusive coaching methods and their harmful implications only intensify as the athlete becomes more successful and more invested in the sport. In a sport like figure skating, where it's not atypical for the elite child athletes to spend more time with their coach than with their parents, the effects of emotional abuse by the coach are similar to the consequences of child abuse in parent-child relationships. Research suggests that negative psychological effects of abusive coach-athlete relationships include low mood, low self-efficacy, anger, low self-esteem, anxiety and poor body image, which are all possible results of abusive parent-child relationships, too. There might be also long-term psychological consequences such as complex PTSD (post-traumatic stress disorder), high-level dissociation, and conflicting love/hate views about emotionally abusive coaches as well as difficulty forming healthy identity and relationships after the athletic career.

Unfortunately, emotional abuse seems to be a widely accepted coaching philosophy, and even though this kind of behavior may be very harmful to the athlete's well-being, it isn't usually challenged as long as the athlete is successful. The athletes might be reluctant to report abusive experiences. Parents, athletes, and other coaches are often present while these damaging behaviors occur, which only adds to the problem of normalization of abuse.

I hope the content of this book has provided a small but much needed glimpse into the minds of former elite child athletes who have been "products" of emotionally abusive coaching systems.

What Next?

Despite the darker realities I've just described, I'm very hopeful for the future. There's a rapidly growing number of people, a new generation of athletes, coaches, officials, parents, journalists, fans and others, who see the problems of the old-fashioned, inhumane system and are not afraid to challenge the status quo.

In coaching, there's a radical evolution happening. The mindset of the 20th century, where we saw people and the world very mechanistically, is being elevated to the 21st-century mindset, where we see people and the world much more holistically. In sports, this means that we see athletes as people first and as athletes second.

Learning and developing a strong community are seen as goals, rather than just having the goal be winning.

It means that in coaching we strive to have a dialogue with the athlete, not a monologue by the coach.

It means that we coach dynamically the whole person—their body, mind and emotions—not just mechanistically the body.

It means that when we coach children, we try to include their own goals and their own feelings and thoughts into the coaching process.

It means that our sport governing bodies strive not only to make sport safe and healthy for all who participate, but to guarantee that sport participation is accessible and affordable to *everyone* and that sports doesn't damage our environment.

The bottom line of the 21st-century sports world is not the number of medals and short-term economic profits but the long-term humanitarian success of individuals and communities. *That* is the sports world I want to live in—a world where children have a say, they have a voice, and they have power to influence decisions that concern them.

Sports has a special way to get into our souls. It can make us feel really alive and inspired and that we belong to each other. That's why I believe that transforming sports can help transform our nations and our world.

In the middle of a circle at Rockefeller Center Rink, 2018.

References

Dietz, C.M., et al. (2015). Development and validation of the coach-athlete relationship emotional maltreatment scale (CAREMS). *Athletic Insight, 7*(3), 209–226.

Gervis, M., & Dunn, N. (2004). The emotional abuse of elite child athletes by their coaches. *Child Abuse Review, 13,* 215–223. *https://doi-org.libproxy.newschool.edu/10.1002/car.843.*

Kirby, S., Greaves, L., & Hankivsky, O. (2002). *Women under the dome of silence: sexual harassment and abuse of female athletes.* Halifax, NS: Fernwood.

Stafford, A., Alexander, K., & Fry, D. (2013). "There was something that wasn't right because that was the only place I ever got treated like that": Children and young people's experiences of emotional harm in sport. *SAGE Journals. https://journals.sagepub.com/doi/10.1177/0907568213505625.*

Stirling, A.E. (2009). Definition and constituents of maltreatment in sport: Establishing a conceptual framework for research practitioners. *British Journal of Sports Medicine, 43*(14).

Epilogue

Stirling, A.E., & Kerr, G.A. (2013). The perceived effects of elite athletes' experiences of emotional abuse in the coach-athlete relationship. *International Journal of Sport and Exercise Psychology, 11*(1), 87–100. *https://doi-org.libproxy.newschool.edu/10.1002/car.843.*

Stirling, A.E., & Kerr, G.A. (2014). Initiating and sustaining emotional abuse in the coach-athlete relationship: An ecological model of vulnerability. *Journal of Aggression, Maltreatment and Trauma, 23*(2).

Index

Index